DIMENSIONS:
Literary and Theological

incorporating the St Mary's Lectures
1991-92

DIMENSIONS:
Literary and Theological

(Founded in 1538)

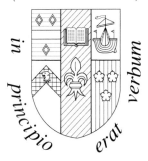

**incorporating the St Mary's Lectures
1991-92**

Edited by D. W. D. Shaw

Grateful acknowledgement is made for permission to reprint extracts from David Jones' *In Parenthesis* and *The Anathemata* in Chapter IV and to the publishers Faber & Faber Ltd.

Published 1992 by

St Mary's College
University of St Andrews
Fife KY16 9JU
Scotland

ISBN 0 9516136 1 8
Copyright © St Mary's College 1992

Designed, typeset and printed by

University of St Andrews Reprographic Services

CONTENTS

Introduction

'If you want our <u>Weltanschauung</u>, I told him, look to our novels, not to our pure thought.' - Ernesto Sabato[1]

Theology is a discipline in its own right. It has its own subject matter, its own categories, its own method, so much so that in the past and still, in some perspectives at least, in the present it claims to be a science, even the Queen of the Sciences! This does not, however, mean that it is self-contained, shut off from other disciplines. On the contrary, it has never functioned effectively without a partner.

Traditionally, theology's consort has been philosophy in one or other of its guises. Thus it is only a slight exaggeration to suggest that the great Augustine would have been a non-starter without Neo-Platonism, as would Thomas Aquinas without Aristotle, most of nineteenth and twentieth century theologians without Kant or Hegel, or latterly Wittgenstein or Whitehead.

Yet philosophy has not been the only partner. Psychology, for example, has proved a valuable resource for the theologians. One of the ironies of twentieth-century theology is the extent to which Sigmund Freud, one of the greatest of reductionists, explaining religion and with it theology away in naturalist, psychological terms, has provided the data for constructive theology. Perhaps even more influential in recent years has been the discipline of sociology, despite or even perhaps because of the reductionist work of the pioneer Emile Durkheim. Twenty years ago, one 'Liberation' theologian opined that the social sciences - he had Karl Marx especially in mind - had now become one of the major theological complements.[2]

What, however, should have been obvious from the start but has often been overlooked is the theological potential of literature. After all, in the Christian tradition, part of the enduring power of the Bible has beeen due to its poetic or literary quality - mention need only be made of the Psalms, or the parables, or the thirteenth chapter of St Paul's First Letter to the Corinthians. Augustine with his *Confessions*, Dante, Milton, John Bunyan, Coleridge, Tolstoy, T.S.Eliot - these and many, many more with their literary creations have, in their own way, made an irreplaceable contribution to the theological enterprise, earthing theology in 'real life' and communicating it in a way denied to most theologians (unless they were also poets or dramatists). Most typically, where would the preacher have been in the first half of this century if he had not been able to resort to Browning or Tennyson for illustration?

---

[1] *The Angel of Darkness*, tr Andrew Hurley, Jonathan Cape, London (1992), p. 194

[2] cf Gustavo Gutierrez, *A Theology of Liberation,* SCM Press, London (1973), pp. 5, 9.

At last this potential has begun to be appreciated not simply as a reservoir of sermon illustrations, but as offering genuine insight into truly theological questions. The perception of such contemporary 'critic-theologians' as Nathan Scott[1] in America or D.Z.Phillips[2] in Britain or René Girard[3] in France - to cite three names at random - have begun to bear fruit. Theologians are discovering that theological issues can be investigated more profoundly, more intelligibly, indeed more existentially when heed is taken of the insights of poets, novelists and dramatists. Thus no modern discussion of the problem of evil can proceed without taking account of literary treatments such as Ivan's 'Rebellion' in Dostoevsky's *The Brothers Karamazov* [4], or Elie Wiesel's *Night*[5]. 'Creation', so much discussed in these ecologically sensitive days, can be given new immediacy when illumined by the writings, for example, of Annie Dillard[6]; and redemption is an ever-recurring theme in the contemporary novel (not simply the French Catholic novels[7]).

In short, it has become abundantly clear that theology, whatever its emphasis - systematic, apologetic, pastoral - has everything to gain and nothing to lose by paying attention to the contemporary literary world, its creators and interpreters. Literary criticism can merge into valid and original theological comment. The literary dimension is to be ignored at the theologian's peril.

What is not so often appreciated is that the corollary is also true. It has sometimes been too easily assumed that appreciation of literature could be full, accurate and responsible without any real understanding or serious consideration of religious or theological questions or attitudes. It could be said that this is one of the asssumptions which this volume seeks to query - the other, already alluded to, being that literature has nothing to teach theology. Just as the literary dimension cannot be ignored in theology, so in literary appreciation and analysis, the theological or religious dimension can offer important insights and suggestive interpretations.

---

[1] e.g. *The Broken Centre*, Yale University Press,New Haven (1966); *Craters of the Spirit*, Sheed & Ward, London (1969)

[2] e.g. *Through a Darkening Glass*, Basil Blackwell, Oxford (1982) See also T.R.Wright, *Theology and Literature*, Basil Blackwell, Oxford, (1981)

[3] e.g. *The Scapegoat*, John Hopkins University Press, Baltimore, (1986); *A Theatre of Envy: William Shakespeare*, Oxford University Press, (1991)

[4] Vol. I, Bk. 5, c. 4, Penguin Books (1971) London, pp.276 - 288

[5] Hamilton & Co., London (1961)

[6] e.g. *Pilgrim at Tinker Creek*, Pan Books Ltd., London (1976); *Teaching a Stone to Talk*, Pan Books Ltd., London (1984)

[7] cf ch. VII.

For example, while it is generally acknowledged that Nietzsche has been one of the decisive influences on European thought and literature in the twentieth century, his real understanding of the 'Death of God' and, of course, 'the Superman', have been disastrously misrepresented. R.S. Furness effectively redresses the balance. Would that his insights had been available to the 'Death of God' theologians of the 'sixties' and 'seventies'! Three contrasting attitudes to religion and theology in British literature are offered.Theological sensitivity enables Phillip Mallett to give a singular interpretation of 'that vast compendium of 19th century thought',[1] Tennyson's *In Memoriam*; Peter Coxon draws extensively on Thomas Hardy's poetry to elucidate Hardy's far from simple attitude to Christian faith and the Church; and Michael Alexander takes as his subject a soldier-poet, the Welshman David Jones, with his distinctive and distinctively Christian interpretation of the First World War trench experience.

The field is broadened out internationally to include R.F.Christian's authoritative study of faith and doubt in Dostoevsky, Paul Gifford's researches - yielding results, to many, new and surprising - into Paul Valéry, and Malcolm Scott's consideration of the French Catholic novelists, writing and succeeding in the heyday of agnosticism and secularism.

The contributors to this volume are all teachers at the University of St Andrews, all acknowledged authorities on the authors of whom they write. With the exception of Philip Mallett's piece (included here for its obvious relevance - and quality), all the chapters were delivered as lectures at St Mary's College ('St Mary's College Lectures', 1991 and 1992) under the general title *Theology and Literature*, the lecturers choosing their own particular subject. The popularity of these lectures proved the helpfulness of exploring on the one hand the theological presuppositions behind great literature, and on the other the genuine theological resource which literature provides. To avoid artificiality, the lecture form has been retained. As editor, I am most grateful to my colleagues for allowing their lectures to be included here, in what is intended as a small contribution to the ongoing and important dialogue between literary critics and theologians.

St Andrews, 1992   D.W.D. Shaw

---

[1] *The Cambridge Guide to Literature in English,* (ed. Ian Ousby) , Cambridge (1988), p.979˙

I *Nietzsche, the Madman and the Death of God*

For Erich Heller (1911-1990)

– R. S. Furness

It would be appropriate to begin this paper with a quotation by Erich Heller written in *Encounter* in April 1964, a statement on the importance of Nietzsche. Heller begins by describing the indebtedness of modern European thought to German thinkers and writers - he explains as follows:

> Defeated in two world wars, Germany appears to have invaded vast territories of the world's mind, with Nietzsche himself as no mean conqueror. For his was a vision of things to come. Amongst all of the thinkers of the nineteenth century he is, with the possible exception of Kierkegaard and Dostoevsky, the only one who would not be too amazed by the amazing scene upon which we now move in sad, pathetic, heroic, stoic or ludicrous bewilderment. Much, too, would strike him as *déja-vu*:; he had foreseen it and he would understand: for the modern mind speaks German, not always good German, but fluent German nonetheless. It was, alas, forced to learn the idiom of Karl Marx, and was delighted to be introduced to itself in the language of Sigmund Freud; taught by Ranke and, later, Max Weber, it acquired its historical and sociological self-consciousness, moved out its tidy Newtonian universe on the instruction of Einstein, and followed a design of Oswald Spengler's in sending from the depth of its spiritual depression most ingeniously engineered objects higher than the moon. Whether it discovers, with Heidegger, the true habitation of its *Existenz* on the frontiers of Nothing, or meditates, with Sartre and Camus, le Néant or the Absurd; whether - to pass to its less serious moods - it is nihilistically young and profitably angry in London or rebelliously debauched and buddhistic in San Francisco - *man spricht deutsch*. It is all part of a story told by Nietzsche.[1]

A figure of immense importance, then, and there is hardly a major figure in modern German intellectual life who is not indebted to Nietzsche; in some cases we might

---

[1] Encounter, April 1964, p.59. (Reprinted in *The Importance of Nietzsche. Ten Essays,* University of Chicago Press, 1988).

even claim that they would not have been what they are if Nietzsche had not lived. We think of Rilke and his later work, of Stefan George, of Franz Kafka, of the Expressionists, of Thomas Mann and *Doktor Faustus*, of Hermann Hesse and *Das Glasperlenspiel*, of Robert Musil, of Gottfried Benn, of Heidegger and Jaspers. Many overtly acknowledge his influence, the influence of that writer who, for Gottfried Benn, was 'the ubiquitous giant of the post-Goethe epoch'.[1] And not only Germany is indebted: the major writers and thinkers of Europe and North America stand beneath the awesome shadow which he has cast.[2] As Heller put it: he is to modern writers what St. Thomas Aquinas was to Dante - the categorical interpreter of a world which they contemplate poetically or philosophically without ever radically upsetting its Nietzschean structure.

Nietzsche died in 1900 after almost twelve years of insanity: daunting indeed that the new century - his century, we might say - should have a stricken poet-philosopher as its godfather. That most remarkable autobiography *Ecce Homo*, written in a hectic euphoria with its sections 'Why I am so wise', 'Why I am so clever', 'Why I write such good books' and 'Why I am a man of destiny' shows a mind in febrile incandescence, a lurid, moving and often desperate attempt to plot a fever chart, or, rather, to demonstrate that there is no disease, only an act of affirmation and praise. 'In the anticipation that I will soon impose upon mankind the most difficult task that it has ever had to bear it seems incumbent on me to say *who I am.*'[3] This is the opening statement: he is also convinced, he tells us, that it would take some fifty years before a few men might understand what he had accomplished; and he feared that even then his teaching would be misinterpreted or misapplied. Like that thinker envisaged in his early essay *Schopenhauer as Educator* 'he will be misunderstood, and for a long time thought to be an ally of those he abhors'[4], terrified, indeed, by the thought of the sort of person who might one day invoke his authority. His path will become one of increasing isolation, the growing shrillness and heady euphoria resulting from the knowledge that there was a danger in his thinking made necessary by the deepest insights, a fascinating spell which would be cast over the finest as well as the coarsest minds.

---

[1] *Gesammelte Werke* in 8 Bänden, Wiesbaden, 1962, IV, 1046.

[2] For Nietzsche's influence on German literature see *Nietzsche und die deutsche Literatur*, 2 vols, Tübingen, 1978; on Britain and North America see Patrick Bridgwater, *Nietzsche and Anglosaxony*, Leicester, 1972; on Nietzsche and the French see W.D. Williams, *Nietzsche and the French*, Oxford 1952; on Nietzsche and Russia see B. Glatzer-Rosenthal (ed.), *Nietzsche in Russia*, Princeton, 1986.

[3] Friedrich Nietzsche. *Werke* in drei Bänden (ed. Karl Schlechta), Hanser, Munich, 1954, Vol. II, 1065. This edition, abbreviated *W,* will be used throughout, English translation being the author's.

[4] *W* . I, 318.

The fact that so many writers, artists, thinkers and musicians in our century have acknowledged him as a mentor is an indication that he is not simply to be understood as a man who found it necessary to attack the fashionable concerns of his day, a gadfly, as it were, on the neck of the nineteenth century. What makes him such a forbidding as well as a fascinating figure is that awareness which singles him out from contemporary polemics, a discovery which, if you like, serves him as a lever to unhinge the whole fabric of traditional values.

It is the knowledge that 'Gott ist tot'.

The death of God, as we shall see, is for Nietzsche the greatest event in human history - but also the cause of extreme danger. This is no mere atheism, but an agonizing awareness of what the end of religious faith will mean: its announcement is, to turn to Heller once more, 'a cry mingled of despair and triumph, reducing, by comparison, the whole history of atheism and agnosticism before and after him to the level of respectable mediocrity and making it sound like a collection of announcements of bankers who regret they are unable to invest in an unsound proposition.'[1] It may be argued here that Nietzsche belongs in a tradition of religious thought - together with Kierkegaard and Pascal (of the latter, particularly, he has much to say) which may be called 'existentialist' in that God is seen not so much as a creator of some divine order, but as the very ground of Being itself, a presence beyond reason, a constant challenge. It is a great pity that Nietzsche did not have the opportunity to tackle the writings of Kierkegaard (a letter of 19th February 1888 to Georg Brandes refers to him and to his desire to get to grips with Kierkegaard as a psychological problem[2]): Kierkegaard's awareness of a discontinuity between faith and reason, his rejection of speculative philosophy (particularly Hegel) and the concept of Christian faith as being wholly alien to reason and experience, incapable of assimilation, as a provocation, would have fascinated him. Nietzsche may be seen as that nineteenth century thinker who devoted his life to exploring that whole contrast to what may be called a truly religious life, knowing the Devil, as it were, and all his visions of God.

'Gott ist tot' - this is the very core of Nietzsche's spiritual existence, and his writing reverberates with the passion of a thinker who was forever rent by a desperate desire to uphold that against which he must needs turn the icy brilliance of his intellect. So it is no coincidence that Nietzsche greatly admired the German Romantic poet Friedrich Hölderlin (1770-1843), particularly the latter's visionary, unfinished

---

[1] Heller, loc. cit., p.60.

[2] *W*, III, 1278.

drama on Empedocles; the philosophical essay *Der Grund zum Empedokles*, which stresses the need for a reconciliation of opposites, may also have been known to Nietzsche. Nietzsche's plans for his own Empedokles tells of one who has passed through the spheres of religion and art and who turns the weapon of his intellect against his earlier illusions: originally full of love, he is broken on the wheel of existence and, insane, destroys himself. The professor of Classical Philology had spoken in academic and sober terms of Empedocles in his course of lectures on Pre-Socratic philosophy at Basle during the summer term of 1872: the poet sensed that Empedocles was somehow a precursor whose legendary life and death provided an uncanny anticipation of his own position.

Let us now look at that infamous pronouncement of God's death in *The Joyful Science (Die fröhliche Wissenschaft)*, 1882. A brief reminder of Nietzsche's career till then: in 1879 he had resigned from the post of Professor of Classical Philology at the University of Basle; he was then thirty five years old. This brilliantly precocious son of the manse had astounded and infuriated the academic world with his first book *The Birth of Tragedy from the Spirit of Music (Die Geburt der Tragödie aus dem Geist der Musik)* of 1872, an extraordinary description of the Dionysian element in Greek art and an unrestrained advocacy of the work of Richard Wagner, in whose music-drama Nietzsche had then seen a rebirth of the tragic spirit. Attacked by fellow classicists for the dazzling extravagance of his thought, and sickened by what he felt to be Wagner's prostitution before the blandishments of commercial success at Bayreuth, Nietzsche acknowledged that his own path was to be one of loneliness and untrammelled freedom. Between 1879 and his mental collapse in January 1889 Nietzsche made frequent changes of residence, living in the lonely and lovely valley of Sils Maria in the Oberengadin, in the south of France, and in Italy. In increasing isolation he sought to look with psychologicial rigour at the whole history of inherited and contemporary ideas and values, sensing that man's reluctance to question and understand traditional evaluation would soon be overtaken by an enormous bankruptcy. The next substantial work, *Human, All-too Human (Menschliches Allzumenschliches)* appeared in two parts, 1878-80, an apparently complete break with Wagner, with Schopenhauerian metaphysics, with the German Romantic tradition: *Dawn of Day (Morgenröte)* (1881) continued the attack on traditional concepts and extolled the Freier Geist. He seeks, he tells us here, to force men to leave pusillanimous acceptance and to flee into the mountains, the high places, away from the swamp of prejudice and moribund obedience. A gaya scienza is sought, a new freedom and vision: *Die fröhliche Wissenschaft*, (1882) is a book both subjective and lyrical, aphoristic (there are some 380 of them) and deeply personal. Nietzsche faces - as we know - the profoundest question of all, the question concerning the consequences of God's death. The aphorism (no. 125) - or, rather, rhapsodic utterance - is entitled *Der tolle Mensch (The Madman)*:

Have you not heard of that madman who, in the broad light of the forenoon, lit a lantern and ran into the marketplace crying incessantly: 'I am looking for God! I am looking for God!' As it so happened that there were many standing around who did not believe in God, he caused much hilarity. 'Has he got lost?' asked one. 'Has he run away like a child?' asked another. 'Or is he hiding?' 'Is he frightened of us? Has he gone on board ship? Emigrated?' - so they yelled and laughed in uproar. The madman leapt straight amongst them and transfixed them with his gaze. 'Where has God gone - I shall tell you. *We have murdered Him* - you and I. But how did we do this deed? How did we drink the ocean dry? Who gave us the sponge with which to wipe out the whole horizon? How did we set about unchaining the earth from her sun? Whither is it moving now? Whither are *we* moving? Are we not falling incessantly? Away from all suns? Backwards, sideways, forwards - in all directions? Is there still an Above and a Below? Are we not wandering as through an empty Nothingness? Do we not feel the breath of empty space? Has it now grown colder? Is night not approaching, and more and more night? Must we not light lanterns in the forenoon? Do we not hear the noise of the gravediggers busy to bury God? Do we not smell the divine putrefaction? - Gods also decay! God is dead! God will stay dead! And we have killed Him! What possible comfort is there for us, the greatest of murderers? That which was the holiest, the most powerful that the world ever possessed: it has bled to death beneath our knives. And who washes this blood from us? With what waters can we purify ourselves? What atonements, what holy rituals must we not invent? Is not the greatness of this deed too great for us? Must we not become gods ourselves in order to be worthy of this deed? There never was a greater deed - and he who is born after us belongs because of this deed in a higher history than any history was until now!' Here the madman fell silent and looked at his audience: they too were silent and looked at him in bewilderment. Finally he threw his lantern to the ground, where it shattered and extinguished. 'I have come too early', he said 'My time has not yet come. The news of this tremendous event is still on its way - it has not reached the ears of men. Lightning and thunder need time, the light of the stars needs time, deeds need time, even after they have been accomplished, to be seen and heard. This deed is still farthest from them than the farthest stars - *and yet it was they themselves who did it!* [1]

---

[1] *W* , II, 126-127.

With appalling clarity the madman sees what the end of religious faith will mean: all absolute standards are destroyed, and man is faced with the enormous task of re-interpreting all the traditional evaluations placed upon life. The story of the madman, written two years before *Zarathustra*, shows the distance that divides Nietzsche from the conventional attitudes of atheism. He is the madman, breaking with his sinister views into the market-place complacency of the pharisees of unbelief. They have done away with God, and yet the report of their own deed has not yet reached them. They know not what they have done, but He who could forgive them is no more. Much of Nietzsche's later work is the prophecy of their fate: 'The waters of religion', he will write in the third of his *Untimely Considerations (Unzeitgemässe Betrachtungen)* 'recede, and leave behind morasses and shallow pools...'[1]: Where we live, apparently, soon nobody will be able to exist. To return to *The Joyful Science*, a further aphorism (no. 285) explains yet again what the death of God will mean: 'You will pray no more, you will never more take rest in infinite trust... You do not permit yourself to stand before an absolute Wisdom, absolute Goodness, absolute Power... There is no purpose in that which happens, no love in that which happens to you...'[2] A few years later Nietzsche will single George Eliot out for particular scorn as, in his eyes, she represented that earnest - and completely misguided - Victorian attempt to reject God and yet keep Christian morality, that flabby humanism which, he saw, was a tepid and pusillanimous thing. The paragraph, in *The Twilight of the Idols (Götzendämmerung)* runs as follows: 'George Eliot. They have got rid of the Christian God and believe they must clutch hold of Christian morality even more tightly: this is an Anglo Saxon logical consistency and we must not be too incensed about these moral spinsters à la Eliot... But for us it is different. If one gives up the Christian faith, then one also takes away from oneself the right to Christian morality... This is not self-apparent, and one must ignore the English cretins here and bring this truth into the light of day. Christianity is a system, a compounded and compact view of things. If one removes a central concept, for example the belief in God, then the whole system falls to pieces...'[3] One wonders what Nietzsche père, the Saxon Lutheran pastor, would have said here!

Our madman sees that with the death of God there is no longer an absolute, be it goodness, truth or love: what remains is a vision of life in all its nakedness, urgency and power, life at its most fundamental and amoral, stripped of all the categories and evaluations that we have placed upon it. With the collapse of any divine sanction

---

[1] *W*, I. 312. 10.

[2] *W*, II, 166.

[3] *W*, II, 992.

Nietzsche feels that the value of any belief - and his philosophy, if philosophy it is, is fundamentally a transvaluation of all values (or '*Umwertung aller Werte*') will now be determined from the standpoint of whether or not it furthers life in this godless, amoral or 'Dionysian' sense - this latter term he had used in *The Birth of Tragedy* where the Greek deity is extolled as a dark, counter-pole to the Apolline, to harmony and order, the transmuted Schopenhauerian Will and the very ground of being itself. So 'true' is that which now promotes existence - existence interpreted as an ubiquitous Will to Power - and even that which had been 'false' in the conventional sense of the term may be hailed as 'good' if it is life-enhancing. In the book which followed his dithyrambic prose poem *Also sprach Zarathustra*, in *Beyond Good and Evil* (*Jenseits von Gut und Böse*) (1886), a preparation for his intended, but never completed, masterpiece *The Will to Power* (*Der Wille zur Macht*), Nietzsche explains: 'The falseness of a judgement is for us certainly no objection to this judgement: perhaps our new language sounds strangest here. The question is asked: whether or not the judgement promotes life, maintains life...'[1] And such a view, Nietzsche knows, is startling, and he who holds it lays the axe at man's traditional concepts. 'To admit falseness as a condition of life: this means indeed opposing the traditional evaluations in a dangerous way, and a philosophy which dares do this places itself simply *by* doing this beyond good and evil.'[2] A dangerous path indeed, and one which will lead Nietzsche into an ever-increasing isolation and final mental disintegration. For the fascinating agony of his thought is the knowledge that there is no absolute truth if the Christian God is rejected, and that therefore his own 'Dionysian' vision can lay no claims to absolute validity. Hence Nietzsche rends himself, and the quality of his thought assumes an unprecedented poignancy.

What makes Nietzsche so fascinating - and to some so irritating - is the number of obvious paradoxes running through his work. Unable to stand firmly upon the principle of amoral life-affirmation (for there is no universally valid injunction any more), Nietzsche questions his own 'truth' by turning the knife-edge of his thought against himself. A 'Dionysian' concept is posited - for example, that man has conquered all fear of nihilism caused by subservience to some spiritual sanction - yet almost at once its opposite is put forward. On the one hand there is a more refined sense of truth than any other civilisation has ever known, an almost uncontrollable desire for absolute intellectual certainities - yet also an ever present suspicion that life on this earth, despite Zarathustra's dithyrambs, is not in itself of supreme value, but stands in the need of a higher, transcendental justification. Beneath the sound

---

[1] *W*, II, 569.

[2] *W*, II, 569-570.

and fury of the Superman's utterances - the praise of Life, Earth, Energy, Sunrise, Midday, Joy, Power and a host of other ringing ecstasies - there is Nietzsche's quieter voice, querying and questioning the intellectual violence. He specifically warns us *not* to take sides with him, but to think, criticise, doubt. In a letter dating from 1888 he explains the following:- 'It is by no means necessary, not even desirable, to take my side in all this: indeed, a dose of curiosity, as before a rather strange plant, with an ironic spirit of opposition, would seem to me to be an incomparably more intelligent attitude to take.'[1] In another letter, this time to his friend Overbeck written at the time of *Zarathustra*'s completion, when Nietzsche's 'Dionysian' life-affirmation was at its most intense and visionary, he wonders whether his amoralism and repudiation of conventional morality were, in fact, as valuable and as dynamic as he had once believed: 'My life now consists in the desire that all things might be *different* from my understanding of them and that somebody would make my "truths" impossible to believe in.'[2] We remember his feeling of dread, of terror even, at the sort of people who might one day invoke his authority. And Zarathustra himself warns us not to follow: we must be on our guard against him, for even he may deceive. The end of Book 1 contains the following warning: 'Now, my disciples. I go alone. Go ye also now, and alone. This is my wish. Verily I say unto you: go forth from me, and arm yourselves against Zarathustra. And better still: be ashamed of him. Perhaps he deceived you. You believed in me, but what are believers to me...?'[3]

Zarathustra asks us not to believe him, as Nietzsche himself admitted that he had spent all his days in philosophically *taking sides against himself*. It seems that beneath the sound and fury of *Zarathustra*, beneath the great shouts and imperious proclamations Nietzsche's hesitations are quietly yet insistently stated. *His* Empedocles could not embrace and reconcile the conflicts of his age: he becomes ruthless, misanthropic and finally insane. Nietzsche himself is unable to follow Zarathustra or any other *Ja-sager* : the view of the totality of life beyond good and evil needs a stronger and less sensitive prophet.

How far could we believe in the truth of his writings? In this strange conflict he attacked that which was latent within himself - Schopenhauerian pessismism, Wagnerian Romanticism and also Christianity. Yet could he believe his own critique? Are his ideas not merely experiments to test his as well as his readers' reactions? If there *is* no ultimate truth, then can Nietzsche's apostasy be genuine?

---

[1] *W*, III, 1308.

[2] Friedrich Nietzsche, *Briefwechsel mit Overbeck*, p.155 (2 July 1885).

[3] *W*, II, 339 and 340.

Is it not perhaps a mask which he assumes in order to take sides against himself? It has already been regretted that Nietzsche's awareness of Kierkegaard came too late. For like Kierkegaard, who is both the aesthete in love with life and the religous thinker who sees the ethical need for Christianity, and like Dostoevsky (and here Nietzsche *did* admit an admiration for the Russian novelist) who is at once Mitya, Ivan and Alyosha Karamazov, Nietzsche preaches respect for the mask, and the philosopher with the hammer who feels driven to bring down the whole edifice of European metaphysics and morality can also extol - if not obey - the highest Christian injunction. Paragraph 60 of *Jenseits von Gut und Böse* runs as follows: 'To love man *for the sake of God* - this has been the most refined and recondite emotion ever pronounced holy amongst mankind. That love for man, without a sanctifying ulterior motive, is simply another stupidity and bestiality, that this tendency to love man has to receive its measure of refinement, its grain of salt and speck of amber from a higher tendency - whoever it was who first felt and "experienced" this, let him remain, however much his tongue may have stammered as it tried to express such a senstive awareness, let him remain for all time holy and laudable as that man who has flown the highest - and who erred in the most beautiful way!'[1]

The prophet of Dionysus can admire and praise the example of Christ, even though Christ and Dionysus are locked in bitter conflict. For if there is no absolute standard of truth one cannot condemm or praise any particular view according to its 'rightness': one can, however, admire the quality of mind from which such a view has sprung. There is, for Nietzsche, a dichotomy between the thinker and the views he expresses: of himself he writes - 'I am one thing, and my writings are another'[2] (this is the beginning of the section 'Why I write such good books' from *Ecce Homo)*. This explains Nietzsche's great admiration for a man like Pascal, whose views seem diametrically opposed to his own, yet the quality of whose mind is matched only perhaps by Nietzsche's itself, and his contempt for the theologian David Friedrich Strauss, author of the *Leben Jesu* (1835), whose destructive, demythologizing method strikes one as mediocre and completely lacking the passionate intensity and complexity of Nietzsche's own critique. (Nietzsche singles out the complacency of Strauss for particular vituperation: it was impossible for him to believe, as Strauss did, that the tenets of religion could be rejected and for life to continue as if nothing had changed - for everything had changed, and changed utterly). It seems that Nietzsche sought worthy opponents, and sought those figures who had written, composed and thought before him against whom to measure himself: 'To circle the complete circumference of the modern soul, to have sat in each of its corners - this is my ambition, my agony, my joy ...'[3]

---

[1] *W*, II, 620-621.

[2] *W*, II, 1099.

[3] *W*, III, 512.

Nietzsche is trapped in a vicious circle, and the brilliance of his thought is, in fact, a self-inflicted agony. He is unable to eradicate traditional Christian concepts, and the paradox of his own thinking springs ultimately from his inability to separate the idea of God from that of absolute Truth. Morality itself, refusing to be deceived, cannot allow the deception of God, and has dispensed with Him - aphorism 357 of *The Joyful Science* explains: 'One sees what it was that triumphed over the Christian God: Christian morality itself, the concept of truthfulness taken increasingly seriously...'[1] Perhaps the godless one is the most pious of all? In the fourth and final section of *Thus spake Zarathustra* the 'godless one', the one who had earlier greeted the sunrise in a transport of ecstasy (so well captured in the music of Richard Strauss), Zarathustra, now wanders through a dark forest and a rocky labyrinth: he comes across a gaunt figure, the old Pope, or, rather, the last Pope, 'der letzte Papst'. This figure addresses Zarathustra thus: 'O Zarathustra, thou art more pious than thou thinkest, with such a lack of faith. Some God in thee it was that converted thee to thy godlessness! Is it not thy piety itself which prevents thee from believing in God? [...] Close to thee, even though thou wouldst be the most godless of men, I sense a secret scent of balsam and of incense: I rejoice and am saddened thereby.'[2] There are echoes here, surely, of the belief that the one who has fallen most deeply is the one who, paradoxically, is closest to God, a theme which Thomas Mann, some sixty years later, will explore in his *Faustus* novel whose hero, Adrian Leverkühn, is modelled very closely upon Nietzsche himself.

Where is the Antichrist in all this, the dynamiting and hammering, the blasting and bombardiering? Nowhere. The Superman is nowhere extolled as a figure of brute force, but that man who has been able to conquer that which was base in himself; the Will to Power likewise has nothing to do with political aggrandizement (how Nietzsche detested Prussian arrogance!) but with the striving to reach true potential; the blonde beast - an unfortunate metaphor - symbolises youth and energy as opposed to moribund slackness. Time and time again we find in the writings of this most remarkable thinker passages of great tenderness, a lull before the storm, perhaps, where he will extol calm, serenity and mature loveliness - the Mediterranean coastline, say, or the music of Bach (one Easter he listens three times to the St Matthew Passion), or the writings of Goethe, Keller and Adalbert Stifter. Far too often Nietzsche is misunderstood as an iconoclast, the philosopher with the hammer who wilfully exults in turbulence and uproar; a more correct assessment is that of the traditionalist who, fearing that nihilism, this most 'uncanny guest',[3] was waiting

---

[1] *W*, II, 227.

[2] *W*, II, 500.

[3] *W*, III, 881.

at the door, sought to preserve the fruits of human culture. There is also, deep down, the awareness that his intellectual probity and refusal to accept the comforts of belief have invited this sinister guest, and that he, Nietzsche, is preparing the way for catastrophe.

The death of God, as we have said, Nietzsche calls the greatest event in modern history: let us remember the Madman's words: 'That which was the holiest, the most powerful thing that the world has ever known - it has bled to death beneath our knives...' What now remains is a senseless universe, devoid of love and purpose, and man, in his heart of hearts, is incapable of forgiving himself for having done away with Him: he is bent upon punishing himself for this, his 'greatest deed'. Morality without religion? Indeed not, as we have seen in the attack against George Eliot: 'All purely moral demands without their religious basis', Nietzsche writes, 'must needs end in nihilism.'[1] What remains? Intoxication? 'Intoxication with music, with cruelty, with hero worship or with hatred... Some sort of mysticism... Art for art's sake, truth for truth's sake, as a narcotic against self-distrust; some kind of routine - *any* silly little fanaticism.'[2] But none of these drugs can have any lasting effect. The time will come, Nietzsche predicts, when the world, unhooked from its divine ground of being, will move into an ever icier darkness, a darkness shot though with lurid detonations and convulsions, as demagogues and false prophets sought to impose their demented visions upon a doomed humanity. And the section 'Why I am a man of destiny' from *Ecce Homo* finishes with a fearful prophecy - that politics now becomes ideology, and that 'there will be wars, the like of which have never been seen on earth.'[3]

What can be put in the place of a nihilistic, godless universe? The Eternal Recurrence of all things is Nietzsche's mythic formulation of a meaningless world, an endless existence with neither hope nor salvation. Nietzsche found the doctrine in the ancient Greeks and resurrects it as a kind of Darwinian test to select for survival the spiritually fittest. The thought of the Eternal Recurrence is, for Nietzsche, the hardest thought of all, and the Superman is meant to be that creature who can accept it lightheartedly and joyously. The Superman, perhaps - yet Zarathustra tells of a supreme act of self-overcoming, of revulsion even, before it was accepted. For the nightmare of nightmares was, for Nietzsche, the idea that he might have to live his identical life again and again, without meaning or goal, inescapably recurrent, without any resolution. We murderers of God must now face

---

[1] *W*, III, 881.

[2] *W*, III, 911

[3] *W*, II, 1153.

the *nihil*, but can we bear the horrifying prospect of godlessness? The penultimate section of book four of *The Joyful Science* is called 'The heaviest burden', and we read: 'Supposing that, one day or night, a demon should creep into your loneliest loneliness and say "This life which you are living and have just lived, you will have to live it once again, and endlessly; there will be nothing new in it, but every pain and every joy and every thought and every sigh and everything small and everything great in your life would have to come again and again and everything in the same sequence - this spider and this moonlight between the trees, and this moment and I myself. The eternal hour-glass of life is turned again and again, and you with it, you tiny speck of sand!" Would you not hurl yourself on the ground, and grind your teeth, and curse the demon who speaks to you in this way? Or have you not perhaps experienced a moment of such tremendous import that you would say: "You are a God, and I have never heard anything more divine!"'[1] Can the Superman transmute barren nihilism into Dionysian affirmation? This was Zarathustra's hope, but Nietzsche knew better. The doctrine of the Eternal Recurrence is a metaphysical nonsense, a desperate remedy, an attempt at substitution: the flood gates are open for innumerable substitutes for religion, some cranky, others ominous. 'Any silly little fanaticism' - this will become the order of the day: no mystery, but blasphemy and sacrilege. Zarathustra, the '*Übermensch*',
were these true visions, or grotesque substitutes for the divine? Could they ever be exemplary? And Nietzsche experiences the terror that he might have helped to bring about the very opposite of what he had desired. If God *is* dead, if morality *is* destroyed, then all certainty is lost; the only solution, then, is madness, madness to sweep away all remorse and doubt and with them the spectre of the Law, the spectre that Nietzsche was never able to banish. And that plea for madness of the visionaries and ecstatics who feared the harrowings of doubt and conscience is terrible in its prophetic intensity:

> So give me madness, you heavenly ones! Madness, that I may finally believe in myself! Give deliria and convulsions, terrify me with frost and fire, sudden lights and darkness, as no mortal man has ever seen before, with roarings and moving shapes; let me howl and whine and weep like a beast - only let me find faith in myself! I am devoured by doubts, for I have killed the Law: the Law terrifies me as a body does a living man, for if I am not *greater* than the Law, then I am the most abject of all... [2]

---

[1] *W*. II, 202

[2] *W*, I, 1024.

II The Heart's Answer: Tennyson and In Memoriam

– Phillip Mallett

On Sunday, 15 September 1833, Arthur Hallam died of apoplexy at Vienna, at the early age of twenty-two. Alfred Tennyson, then twenty-four, was already beset with problems. Following the death of his father in March, 1831, he had left Cambridge without taking his degree. In 1832 one of his brothers, Edward, had been admitted to the insane asylum in York, where he was to die in 1890; another, Charles, with whom he had published his *Poems of Two Brothers* in 1827, had recently begun the opium addiction which was to dog his life for twenty years. His own most recent work, the *Poems* published in 1832, had been savaged by J. W. Croker in the influential *Quarterly Review*. The one hopeful part of his life had come earlier in 1833, when the Hallams at last agreed to recognise the engagement between Arthur and Tennyson's sister, Emily. Now that hope had been snatched away by what the letter informing Tennyson of Hallam's death called 'this unexpected dispensation':

> O what to her shall be the end?
> And what to me remains of good?
> To her, perpetual maidenhood,
> And unto me no second friend.   (VI)

Almost at once Tennyson began to write a series of lyrics in response to the loss of his friend, a man 'as near perfection as mortal man could be', initially without any thought of gathering them into a single poem. In May 1850, two weeks before his own marriage to Emily Sellwood, these lyrics were published as *In Memoriam* : in its final version, a sequence of 131 numbered lyrics in the form of octosyllabic quatrains, rhymed *abba,* together with a Prologue addressed to the 'Strong Son of God, immortal Love', and an Epilogue in the form of an epithalamium celebrating the marriage of another sister, Cecilia, to another friend, Edmund Lushington. The Prologue is dated 1849; the Epilogue is undated, but was presumably written around the time of the marriage, in 1842. Few poems have made their mark so quickly. Even as the Tennysons ended their honeymoon, plans were being made for the fourth edition, and in November, just six months after its first appearance, Tennyson was offered, and accepted, the laureateship. The 'delirious man' of lyric XVI, his reason stunned by grief, had   begun his metamorphosis into the Victorian sage.

Two themes dominate *In Memoriam,* one more personal, one more general. The first is Tennyson's quest for the lost Hallam: a desire for some contact with him, through touch, sight or speech, runs all through the poem. It is this theme that justifies T. S. Eliot's description of *In Memoriam* as 'the concentrated diary of a man confessing himself'. The second, broader theme concerns the meaning of life now, after Hallam's death. For Tennyson, the promise of a life after death was 'the cardinal point of Christianity':

> ...life shall live for evermore,
> Else earth is darkness at the core,
> And dust and ashes all that is. (XXXIV)

But the conviction of personal immortality was hard to sustain in the context of Victorian science. Sir William Herschel had revealed the solar system as no more than a minute part of a vast sidereal universe; more than that, the discovery of the evolution of the stars, together with increasing knowledge of novae and variable stars, seemed to show that this universe was unstable, and that the sun and with it the earth might one day come to an end. Sir Charles Lyell's geology had established that former changes to the surface of the earth were to be accounted for by the operation of those forces still visibly at work in the nineteenth century, and not by such catastrophes as the biblical Deluge, but in doing so Lyell had implied a time-scale so vast that it threatened to shrivel human desires and purposes into insignificance. What Tennyson was later to call the 'terrible Muses' of astronomy and geology seemed to undermine the very project of *In Memoriam*. The traditional motif of pastoral elegy, the picture of Nature mourning in sympathy with the poet, was no longer available in a world where our fate was to be 'blown about the desert dust, / Or seal'd within the iron hills' (LVI). Nor could Tennyson, a young and unsuccessful poet, belonging to a family marked by mental instability, draw on the convention that the fame of the dead man would survive in the songs of the elegist. In later years Tennyson was able to emphasise the representative aspects of *In Memoriam*, describing it to James Knowles as 'rather the cry of the whole human race than mine', but in the weeks and months after Hallam's death he could not be sure that these 'wild and wandering cries, / Confusions of a wasted youth' would ever be formed into an integral poem (Prologue).[1]

The two main quests of the poem lead to two kinds of conclusion. First, Tennyson insists on immortality on the basis of the reasons of the heart which reason doesn't know. This is the burden of lyric CXXIV:

---

[1] T. S. Eliot, 'In Memoriam', in *Selected Essays* 3rd Edition, 1951), p. 334; Hallam Lord Tennyson, *Alfred Lord Tennyson: A Memolr*, 2 vols. (1897), I, 321, reporting his father's comment to Bishop Lightfoot; James Knowles, "Aspects of Tennyson, I & II: A Personal Reminiscence", in the *Nineteenth Century* xxxiii (1893), p. 182. There are numerous discussions of the impact of astronomy and geology on Victorian thought; useful starting-points are provided by Jacob Korg, "Astronomical Imagery in Victorian Poetry", and Dennis R. Dean, "'Through Sclence to Despair': Geology and the Victorians", both in *Victorian Science and Victorian Values: Literary Perspectlves*. edited by James Paradis and Thomas Postlewait (New Jersey, 1985).

> ...like a man in wrath the heart
> Stood up and answered 'I have felt.'

This conviction is not reached easily; it is explored and rejected earlier in the sequence, and is held to at the end only after what seems to be a mystical experience of contact in lyric XCV — though it is not clear, even to Tennyson, exactly what he was in contact with. Second, heartened by this subjectivist answer, Tennyson adopts a new perspective in place of the apparently bleak outlook of Victorian science. The immense tracts of time and space opened up by Herschel and Lyell were to be seen not as pushing God out of creation, but as a preparation for the evolution of species. The processes of natural evolution are in turn seen as parallel to both social progress and spiritual development. Man not only must but can

> Move upward, working out the beast,
> And let the ape and tiger die. (CXVIII)

As an immeasurably superior man, Hallam can be seen as a 'type' or forerunner of what the human race will become in the future. But additionally, Hallam is now a spirit, one who has left the 'lower track' of this earthly life (XLVI) for the 'undiscovered lands' of the life after death (XL). That he can be seen in both these ways allows Tennyson to conflate what are really two distinct ideas: (a) the movement from Victorian man towards the 'crowning race' of the future (Epilogue), and (b) the movement from the mortal, material and therefore limited, towards the immortal, spiritual and therefore complete. Each of these ideas is used to support the other. Evidently argument by analogy, or by the conflation of related but still distinct ideas, cannot amount to proof; but the form of the poem, with its numerous short lyrics, is not designed to manufacture proof, nor does Tennyson believe such proof to be possible. Any dogmatic formulation would be only another of those 'little systems' which 'have their day and cease to be'. Conviction must be an act of 'faith, and faith alone ... / Believing where we cannot prove' (Prologue).

The Epilogue to the poem resumes the two main tenets of faith which Tennyson has so painstakingly established. The poet continues to love Hallam, but knows him now as 'That friend of mine who lives in God', and accepts his death as part of the divine purpose; and the laws which govern the natural world are seen as coherent and progressive, preparing for the 'one far-off divine event / To which the whole creation moves'. Even in the summary form in which they are given here, these are difficult ideas, not easily framed in 'matter-moulded forms of speech' (XCV), and it is one part of the purpose of this paper to explore them more fully. There is however a further purpose. I shall argue that the close of the poem is confused, or at least that it is radically not a Christian poem. What leads Tennyson on from lyric to lyric is the sense of Hallam's lost presence; what he seeks is to recover his own 'proper place' in his friend's 'embrace'. Life is not a prelude to salvation, but a delay designed to render their embrace 'a fuller gain of after bliss' (CXVII). And the means to this is not the risen Christ accepted by faith, but the heart's refusal to give Hallam up. The religion of the poem is, in fact, Tennyson's love for Hallam.

****

Tennyson said that the poem fell into four parts, divided by the three sets of Christmas poems, which clearly echo each other:

And sadly fell our Christmas-eve. (XXX)

And calmly fell our Christmas-eve. (LXXVIII)

And strangely falls our Christmas-eve. (CV)

But there are no sharp transitions in the poem, and elsewhere Tennyson spoke of it as being in nine sections, none of them marked by the second Christmas. However, at least the first part of the poem (up to lyric XXVII) is driven by the sense of physical loss. It opens with a *danse macabre* :

Let Love clasp Grief lest both be drown'd,

Let darkness keep her raven gloss:

Ah, sweeter to be drunk with loss,

To dance with death, to beat the ground... (I)

than to fall into forgetfulness. The dance runs to the tune of the churchyard clock which

Beats out the little lives of men. (II)

The embrace of Love and Grief is echoed as the yew tree of the second lyric 'grasps' at 'the stones / That name the underlying dead'. Gazing at the tree, with its reminder of human life outdone by time, the poet has as it were an inverted mystical experience, a vision not of fulness but of negation:

I seem to fail from out my blood

And grow incorporate into thee. (II)

The tree's roots 'net' the 'dreamless' heads of the dead, wrapping around their bones, and the image of the net is picked up in the third lyric when Sorrow speaks:

'The stars,' she whispers, 'blindly run;

A web is wov'n across the sky;

From out waste places comes a cry,

And murmurs from the dying sun: ... (III)

The web not only recalls the net, but also suggests that the heavens now conceal, rather than reveal, the glory of God. The first lyric asks how a man can comfort himself in grief by knowing that it will ultimately strengthen his mind: how can one

... reach a hand thro' time to catch

The far-off interest of tears? (III)

The vainly reaching hand meets only, it seems, the mocking hands of Nature:

A hollow form with empty hands. (III)

And the music of Nature, to which Love and Grief dance by the time of the
churchyard clock, is only, says Sorrow

     A hollow echo of my own.   (III)

The clock beats, but in IV the heart hardly dares to ask

     'What is it makes me beat so low?'   (IV)

and the web across the heavens reappears as 'clouds of nameless trouble' which
cross the 'darken'd eye' of the elegist (IV). In V the failing heart beat is replaced
by the beat of the poem:

       A use in measur'd language lies;
       The sad mechanic exercise,
   Like dull narcotics, numbing pain.   (V)

These echoes and recapitulations suggest the labyrinthine depth of the poet's
imprisonment in grief, as each new lyric, each promise of a fresh start, sees him
dragged back into the same patterns of thought and feeling. At the same time they
prepare the way for the great seventh lyric:

   Dark house, by which once more I stand
     Here in the long unlovely street,
     Doors, where my heart was used to beat
   So quickly, waiting for a hand,

   A hand that can be clasp'd no more—
     Behold me, for I cannot sleep,
     And like a guilty thing I creep
   At earliest morning to the door.

   He is not here; but far away
     The noise of life begins again,
     And ghastly thro' the drizzling rain
   On the bald street breaks the blank day.

The lyric is a parody of a frustrated social call ('He is not here'), and the familiarity
of the situation adds poignancy to the image of the outstretched hand. Formerly the
poet's heart 'used to beat / So quickly'; now he, rather than Hallam, is a ghost
creeping 'like a guilty thing' in the hours before dawn. Guilty, because that is how
survivors feel; but the phrase may also allude to Wordsworth's 'Ode on Intimations
of Immortality', and those 'high instincts' of immortality before which, Wordsworth
says, our 'mortal nature' will 'tremble like a guilty thing surprised' (1.147-8). This
allusion, if such it is, hints at a hopefulness not yet realised in the poem. So too we

may recognise in 'He is not here' the preface to the 'He is risen' of the synoptic gospels: 'He is not here; for he is risen, even as he said' (Matt. 28:6). Yet even as we sense the allusion, we know that all that is risen here, for the elegist, is the 'noise of life' — not even life, but simply its noise — while the day itself is 'ghastly', one of the meanings of which is 'ghostly'. If there is hope here, it is not yet available to the poet. The last line of the lyric changes the stresses, so that the word 'breaks' seems almost literal, as if the day will fall to pieces rather than begin. And lying behind the whole lyric is the conceit of the body as a house: here, an empty house, with the soul departed, and the eyes / windows 'dark'. It is a profoundly eloquent poem; even in *In Memoriam*, there are few lyrics so finely felt, and so deeply moving.

The next sequence of lyrics follows the ship bringing Hallam's remains back to England. The poet fears another death, by drowning, with 'the hands so often clasp'd in mine' left to 'toss with tangle and with shells' (X) — another version of the dance of death. In imagination he flies to the ship, leaving behind the 'mortal ark' of the body, but like the first bird released by Noah finds nowhere for his spirit to rest, and can only 'circle moaning in the air' (XII): evidently the 'measured language' of the poem cannot always 'numb' his pain. These oscillating moods, of 'calm despair' and 'wild unrest' (XVI), are merely the surface signs of his grief, and the lyrics afford no release for the 'deep self', which changes no more
> ... than some dead lake

> That holds the shadow of a lark
> Hung in the shadow of a heaven.   (XVI)
Lyric XVIII recalls the image of the living mourner as a ghost, as the elegist longs to fall on the dead Hallam and through his lips breathe
> The life that almost dies in me   (XVIII)
— 'almost dies', but has to live on in pain until a firmer mind has been formed by his suffering. Lyric XXII recalls the earlier images of web and net, as the poet reflects how 'the Shadow fear'd of man' had taken Hallam from him:
> And spread his mantle dark and cold,
> And wrapp'd thee formless in the fold.   (XXII)
The best hope that he can find in this first group of lyrics in only that he is still glad to have had Hallam's love:
> 'Tis better to have loved and lost
> Than never to have loved at all.   (XXVII)

Many of the images deployed in this opening sequence return later, usually with subtle changes indicating the poet's gradual acceptance of Hallam's death. This is characteristic of much of Tennyson's verse, which is generally more successful in exploring the nuances of mood and feeling than it is in handling narrative, but it is central to the strategy of *In Memoriam*. The lark which is gloomily only a shadow in a shadowed heaven returns in a Spring song:

> And drown'd in yonder living blue
> The lark becomes a sightless song. (CXV)

— the 'living blue' opposed to the earlier 'dead lake'. The idea of death's mantle is revised in a mellow recollection of times past in LXXXIX, when Hallam is remembered as a guest at the Tennysons' home at Somersby:

> O joy to him in this retreat,
> Immantled in ambrosial dark,
> To drink the cooler air ... (XXXIX)

The image here of Hallam's friends gathered in a circle round him through some 'all-golden afternoon', listening to him read from the Italian poets, both recalls and resists the unhappy circling in the air of Tennyson's mourning spirit in XII.

There is no need to extend the list of examples — every reader will find others — but it is worth emphasising their effect. The reappearance of these images, each time quietly modified, allows Tennyson to suggest simultaneously both stability and change. Beneath the fluctuations of mood of which the poet is so conscious, there is underlying continuity; and in times of apparent stagnation, he is in fact being drawn on through almost imperceptible changes towards that 'firmer mind' which is his goal. In this way Tennyson builds into the very fabric of his poem, at the level of his personal experience, the principle of evolutionary progress which is at another level to become part of his conscious argument. This is a subtle but very powerful procedure. Auden has it that Tennyson was 'undoubtedly the stupidest' of English poets. Perhaps he was; but it would be unwise to approach *In Memoriam* on that assumption.[1]

The lyrics in this opening sequence are essentially love poems, driven on by the sense of loss:

> Tears of the widower, when he sees
> A late-lost form that sleep reveals,
> And moves his doubtful arm, and feels
> Her place is empty, fall like these. (XIII)

---

[1] Both A. Dwight Culler, in *The Poetry of Tennyson* (Yale, 1977) and Tess Coslett, in *The 'Scientific Movement' and Victorian Literature* (Brighton, 1982), see *In Memoriam* as a 'gradualist' poem. and associate this with Lyell's work in geology. W. H. Auden's remark is from his *Tennyson: An Introduction and a Selection* (1946),p. x.

Following the first group of Christmas lyrics, the poem opens out to treat its central theme of loss and separation in relation to time and eternity, focussing on the fears implicit in lyric XXXIV:

> ... life shall live for evermore,
> Else earth is darkness at the core.   (XXXIV)

If there is no promise of immortality, then the only love known on earth will be lust alone, love 'in his coarsest Satyr-shape' (XXXV). Without the conviction of personal immortality, Tennyson could envisage nothing but anarchy and despair. He told friends that he would rather know himself lost eternally than not know that mankind was to be saved eternally, and in a manuscript note to his poem 'Vastness' (1885) he wrote: 'What matters anything in this world without full faith in the Immortality of the Soul and of Love?' The popularity of *In Memoriam* attests that Tennyson was not alone in these anxieties — so too does the surge of interest in spiritualism in the third quarter of the century, with its constant searching for evidence of a *post mortem* existence — but the question of life beyond the grave was for him, as Frederic Harrison noted in the 1870s, a kind of 'cerebral nightmare', which would not let him rest. It is not surprising then that the occasionally consolatory lyrics in this part of *In Memoriam* do not really convince. For example, Tennyson turns away from human understanding ('truth in closest words shall fail') to recall the biblical stories ('truth embodied in a tale'), in particular the evidence given by the Incarnation of a God of Love, and a time when

> ... the Word had breath, and wrought
> With human hands.   (XXXVI)

But these themes are dismissed as beyond his facility as a poet, and the Muses rebuke him as one who has merely 'darken'd sanctities with song'. His province is rather to 'lull with song an aching heart' (XXXVII).[1]

At this stage of the poem, Tennyson has to cling to the 'doubtful gleam of solace' that Hallam's spirit, if spirits care for what happens on earth, will be pleased with his verse (XXXVIII). This kind of speculation is characteristic. Historians of religious thought in the nineteenth century distinguish two main conceptions of heaven. In one, heaven is seen as a state defined by a beatific vision of the deity, or perhaps as a place of everlasting worship, offering a fuller entry into the holiness only dimly experienced in this life. In the other, the emphasis falls on the continuity of personal identity and the restoration of interpersonal relationships. It is this second conception that we now think of as typically Victorian — Dr Arnold of Rugby, for example, prayed that his whole family would be 'transplanted entire

---

[1] Frederic Harrison, *Autobiographic Memoirs*, 2 vols. (1911), II, 103, quoted from Robert Bernard Martin, Tennyson: *The Unquiet Heart* (Oxford, 1980), P.484

from heaven to earth, without one failure' — and it is this idea of the afterlife that governs the following section of *In Memoriam*. The questions raised are those of a lover, all but jealous. Will Hallam, as a spirit, indeed care for his poetry? (XXXVIII) Hallam has already entered the afterlife; will Tennyson therefore be 'evermore a life behind', and never truly reunited with his friend? (XLI) Perhaps Death is after all only a kind of sleep, a 'long trance', and he and Hallam will 'Reawaken' together, their love continuing after death as it has 'here in Time' (XLIII). Dare he hope that Hallam, 'ranging with [his] peers' in heaven, will still have some 'dreamy' memory of his life on earth with Tennyson? (XLIV) The purpose of our mortal life is to establish an individual identity, a sense that "'This is I'"; surely then the dead must retain some memory of their former life, or after death each man would have to 'learn himself anew' (XLV). The faith that in the afterlife each individual will merge into a 'general soul' is too 'vague' and too 'unsweet' to answer the poet's needs; not merely the soul but the form too must be eternal: 'And I shall know him when we meet' (XLVII).[1]

Tennyson's prolonged interrogation of life beyond the grave brings him little comfort. Lyrics LIV-LVI represent the nadir of his faith: 'Behold, we know not anything'. What hope we have is but the 'dream' of an 'infant crying in the night' (LIV). Tennyson was drawn to the position known as universalism, that is, the doctrine that even the worst of sinners would ultimately be saved; as Hallam Tennyson records in his *Memoir*. 'he never would believe that Christ could preach "everlasting punishment"'. In *In Memoriam,* this appears as the human trust that 'not one life shall be destroy'd, / Or cast as rubbish to the void' (LIV). But the evidence of Nature seems to pour scorn on such a faith: 'of fifty seeds / She often brings but one to bear' (LV). The evidence offered by the geologists was still harsher. Charles Lyell wrote on the title page to the second volume of his *Principles of Geology:*

> The inhabitants of the globe, like all the other parts of it, are subject to change. It is not only the individual that perishes, but whole species.

Christ had reassured the disciples that not a sparrow fell to the ground without His Father's knowledge, but in the mid-nineteenth century it seemed that He had failed to account for the dodo and the dinosaur. Tennyson had never been persuaded by Paley's argument from design, but the steadily increasing fossil evidence of extinct species seemed almost persuasive counter-evidence. Man had

---

[1] On ideas of heaven see John Hick, *Death and Eternal Life* (1976), and the third chapter in Michael Wheeler's admirable study, *Death and the Future Life In Victorian Literature and Theology* (Cambrldge, 1990). Dr Arnold ls quoted in Arthur Penrhyn Stanley, *The Life and Correspondence of Thomas Arnold. D.D.*, 2 vols. (9th edition, 1875), I, 191.

> ... trusted God was love indeed,
>   And love Creation's final law—
>   Tho' Nature, red in tooth and claw
>   With ravine, shriek'd against his creed—   (LVI)

but that trust had been misplaced. In 1857 Philip Gosse published *Omphalos* in an attempt to reconcile Genesis and the fossil evidence: just as Adam had been created with a navel, and Eden planted with full-grown trees, so too in every other respect the earth had been formed with the structural character of a planet on which life had long existed; the fossil evidence pointed not to the real history of the earth, but as it were to its putative history. Gosse won few supporters, but the extravagance of his argument is an indication of the disquiet caused by geological investigation. The discovery in 1856 of Neanderthal man only added to the anxiety. Was it, after all, man's fate to be 'seal'd within the iron hills', or — since wind and marine erosion would in time destroy the hills too — to be 'blown about the desert dust'? If so, life was merely 'a dream,/A discord' (LVI).[1]

The first words of the following lyric are 'Peace, come away', and from this moment on in the poem there is a tentative movement towards recovery. It *is* only tentative: thus lyric LXXI records a dream which made 'a night-long Present of the Past / In which we went through summer France', but the next marks the anniversary of Hallam's death, 'When the dark hand struck down thro' time, / And cancell'd nature's best' (LXXII). Gradually, however, the mellower lyrics come to dominate. In LXXXV, Tennyson admits the need for some new companionship, but still yearns for one last meeting with Hallam, 'Spirit to Spirit':

> Descend, and touch, and enter; hear
>   The wish too strong for words to name;
>   That in this blindness of the frame
> My Ghost may feel that thine is near.   (XCIII)

This wish is apparently granted in the trance of lyric XCV, in many respects the pivotal poem of the whole sequence. It describes a summer evening at the Tennysons' home, in ways which recall lyric LXXXIX earlier: then, an 'all-golden afternoon' with Hallam literally present; now, the 'silvery haze of summer' at dusk, with Hallam dead yet, mysteriously, still to be present. The mood is melancholy but serene:

> ... bats went round in fragrant skies,
>   And wheel'd or lit the filmy shapes
> That haunt the dusk ...   (XCV)

---

[1] *Alfred Lord Tennyson: A Memoir.* I,322

26

The skies are 'fragrant', yet the moths 'haunt', and the wheeling movement of the bats recalls Tennyson's homeless spirit 'moaning in the air'. The natural description is typically animated — the moths 'with ermine capes / And woolly breasts and beaded eyes' — yet it suggests the obsessive attentiveness of a distressed mind. The songs sung without Hallam are convivial yet sad, 'old songs that peal'd / From knoll to knoll', and outside the circle formed by the family the 'doubtful dusk' reveals where the cattle 'glimmer'd' in the twilight — ghostly, as well as literal. As the others retire to bed, and 'light after light / Went out', Tennyson feels a 'hunger' for Hallam, and reads over his old letters:

> And strangely on the silence broke
> The silent-speaking words, and strange
> Was love's dumb cry defying change
> To test his worth ...   (XCV)

The words speak silently to Tennyson, who responds with his own 'dumb cry', till he feels

> The dead man touch'd me from the past   (XCV)

and

> The living soul was flash'd on mine.   (XCV)

At that moment he feels his soul 'wound' in Hallam's, and 'whirl'd about' till he comes on, simply, 'that which is', the 'deep pulsations' at the heart of the world, and feels not the change of the geological aeons, but 'Aeonian music': not now the music of his own 'measur'd language', merely numbing pain like a narcotic, but an everlasting music, 'measuring out' or bringing to order 'The steps of Time — the shocks of Chance — / The blows of Death'.

The trance is too intense to last. Speech framed to deal with the material world, the 'matter-moulded speech' which is all the poet has, is inadequate to express 'that which I became', and the moment is 'cancell'd, stricken thro' with doubt'. Back in the physical world, the cattle still glimmer, still 'couch'd at ease' in the fields around, obdurately non-mystical. But then comes a breeze to mark the dawn, and then:

> ... East and West, without a breath,
> Mixt their dim lights, like life and death,
> To broaden into boundless day   (XCV)

— prosaic daylight, but also 'boundless day', uniting life and death in one music as the two half-lights, of late evening and early morning, merge together. Nature, in LVI, had told the poet 'I bring to life, I bring to death', making the boundary between the two states both absolute and arbitrary. But in communing with the 'living soul' Tennyson learns that the boundary can be passed, and that what had formerly seemed the utter opposition of life and death can be resolved into a deeper harmony.

It is this experience that provides the basis for Tennyson's assertions in the later lyrics of personal immortality and a purposeful universe. Henry Sidgwick, a friend of Tennyson's and a fellow member of the Metaphysical Society, said that what he found and valued in *In Memoriam* was 'the ineffaceable and ineradicable conviction that *humanity* will not and cannot acquiesce in a godless world: the "man in men" will not do this, whatever individual men may do'. In Tennyson's own words, if ever he heard a voice say '"Believe no more"',

> A warmth within the breast would melt
> The freezing reason's colder part,
> And like a man in wrath the heart
> Stood up and answer'd, "I have felt". (CXXIV)

This subjectivist argument had been used influentially by Coleridge and Carlyle. Coleridge is predictably elusive, but Carlyle, no less predictably, is direct:

> The evidence to me of God — and the only evidence — is the feeling I have, deep down in the very bottom of my heart, of right and truth and justice. Whoever looks into himself must be aware that at the centre of things is a mysterious Demiurgos — who is God ....

In the final analysis, for Tennyson, as for Carlyle, the heart's assurance is its own authority. The sentiment of belief is also the ground of belief.[1]

The faith of *In Memoriam*, then, is centred on the inward evidence, the answer given by the heart. It remained to show that this faith could accommodate and might even find support in the outlooks and procedures of contemporary science, and in particular in the arguments of the evolutionists. Lyric CXVIII is both eloquent and obscure in trying to do so. It implies two kinds of progress. We are asked first to

> ... trust that those we call the dead
> Are breathers of an ampler day
> For ever nobler ends. (CXXIV)

The suggestion here is of a movement from the human to the spiritual, from the material to the non-material. But Tennyson also speaks of the progress of the earth from its beginning in 'tracts of fluent heat', through 'cyclic storms' — the phrase suggests a reference to the nebular hypothesis — till the moment when

> ... at the last arose the man.

Since that moment man has gone on rising:

> Who throve and branch'd from clime to clime

— and in doing so holds out the promise that he will continue to rise (the word

---

[1] Henry Sidgwick is quoted in *Alfred Lord Tennyson: a Memoir*, I, 302. The Metaphysical society was founded in 1869, and was active through the 1870s; Tennyson attended eleven of the meetings. Carlyle is quoted from Robert Langbaum, 'The Dynamic Unity of *In Memoriam*', in *The Modern Spirit* (New York, 1970), p.58.

'branch'd' seems to refer to the division of humanity into different races, rather than to the mutability of species). The man of the nineteenth century represents not the summit of the process, but only an intermediate stage in it:

> The herald of a higher race,
> And of himself in higher place.

If men will only learn to emulate in their own lives this principle of progress, then both the individual and the race as a whole will continue to 'Move upward, working out the beast', and letting 'the ape and tiger die'.

This is an extraordinarily ambitious lyric: the evolution of the physical world, moral and social progress, and the ascent of the soul are all brought into one poem — virtually, indeed, into a single sentence, running from line 7 to line 25 — and made not only to resemble but even to merge into each other. The logic is hardly compelling. The language reflects the changing levels of different parts of the argument: for example, we are to 'trust' that the dead breathe an ampler day, whereas we have the authority of the scientists for our ideas about the origin of the earth ('They say ...'). Despite the rhythmic assurance with which this central sentence sweeps from a report on the past ('They say...') towards the future implied in the word 'herald', its conclusion proves to depend on a conditional: '*If* so he type this work of time / Within himself ...'. The poem argues for the underlying continuity beneath apparent change, from the 'cyclic storms' of the pre-history of the material world to the 'ampler day' and 'nobler ends' which are our spiritual destiny, but its first stanza makes matter and spirit sharply antithetical ('Nature's earth and lime', 'human love and truth'). It closes with the exhortation, 'Arise', which seems to echo but in fact changes the sense of the earlier 'till man arose': 'Arise' means 'ascend', 'arose' means simply 'appeared', and the evident shift between the two senses opens up to the reader precisely the distinction between the two ideas, of evolutionary progress and of evolutionary process, which the poem is trying to muffle or elide.

Intense, eloquent, as it is, lyric CXVIII is finally an uncertain and even an unsatisfactory poem. It seems however to have satisfied Tennyson, since it is followed by a lyric written as a pendant to VII ('Dark house, by which once more I stand'). No longer racked by guilt, the poet is able to stand calmly before his friend's house, and leave with a sense of peace:

> And in my thoughts with scarce a sigh
> I take the pressure of thine hand.   (CXIX)

Confident now that Hallam was not lost to him, and with his faith in a purposeful universe restored, Tennyson was able to shape *In Memoriam,* as he explained to James Knowles, 'into a sort of Divine Comedy, cheerful at the close'. It ends with the Epithalamium written to celebrate his youngest sister's marriage: a wedding to answer a funeral, and the promise of a new life to answer the death at the beginning of the poem. In the infant who will one day spring from the marriage Tennyson sees the promise of a future in which all of mankind will be as Hallam had already been. His sister's child will be 'a closer link / Betwixt us and the crowning race' of which Hallam, 'That friend of mine who lives in God', had provided the 'type', and its birth will mark another step nearer to that

> ... one far-off divine event,
> To which the whole creation moves.   (Epilogue)

****

I suggested that *In Memoriam* is not a Christian poem: that it does not move to faith in God through acceptance of Christ crucified, but rather through love of Hallam to a faith that human love itself is an absolute. In lyric XCVII Tennyson imagines his soul as a wife loving 'darkly', but with a faith which 'is fixt and cannot move', a husband whose understanding far exceeds her own. Behind this lies Paul's account of love in I Corinthians 13: 'For now we see through a glass, darkly; but then face to face: now I know in part; but then shall I know even as I am known.' But what is loved in Tennyson's lyric is Hallam, the husband to the poet's soul, and what will one day be known fully to him is Hallam: till then

> 'I cannot understand: I love.'   (XCVII)

The Prologue, written in 1849 and possibly intended to reassure his future wife of his faith, seems more orthodoxly Christian. Addressed to the 'Strong Son of God, immortal Love', it is a prayer for the advance of human understanding ('knowledge ... of things we see') under the guidance of wisdom:

> Let knowledge grow from more to more,
> But more of reverence in us dwell.   (Prologue)

The distinction between knowledge, implicitly secular, and wisdom, based on the capacity for reverence, was frequently made. It was fundamental to a Romantic theorist like Carlyle that 'Thought without Reverence is barren', mere 'Attorney-Logic' which could never reach to Truth; but even a scientific writer like John Tyndall was at pains to distinguish between the 'knowing' and the 'creative' faculties, thus allowing the scientists on the one hand and the artist or theologian on the other each to delimit their territory. In lyric CXIV Tennyson returns to the topic. The search for knowledge is to continue — 'Let her work prevail' — but knowledge is 'earthly of the mind' and can only truly advance under the tutelage of wisdom, which is 'heavenly of the soul'. This seems merely to echo the Prologue, but the lyric concludes with a prayer not to the 'Strong Son of God' but to Hallam:

> I would the great world grew like thee,
> > Who grewest not alone in power
> > And knowledge, but by year and hour
> In reverence and charity.   (CXIV)

The role given here to Hallam parallels to a remarkable degree that of Christ in the Prologue, as the mediator through 'reverence and charity' between human knowledge and heavenly wisdom. And there are other parallels, no less striking, in these later lyrics. Tennyson's image for the relation of knowledge to wisdom is that of a child holding up a hand to be guided:

> A higher hand must make her mild,
> > ... and guide
> > Her footsteps, moving side by side
> With wisdom, like the younger child.   (CXIV)

In CIX, Tennyson tells us of his friend that 'the child would twine / A trustful hand, unask'd, in thine'. This lyric as a whole is a celebration of Hallam's wisdom, leading to the poet's plea that Hallam's example will 'make me wise': a close echo of the prayer addressed to Christ in the Prologue, 'And in thy wisdom make me wise'. In CX, Hallam is remembered as a young man imparting wisdom to others, including those of 'riper years', like Christ instructing the elders in the Temple (Luke 2:46-7):

> Nor cared the serpent at thy side
> To flicker with his double tongue   (CX)

with again a biblical reminiscence. In the earlier editions, Tennyson describes himself here as 'thy dearest', with perhaps a suggestion of the beloved disciple (the reading 'thy nearest' was adopted in the 1875 edition). The suggestion is made more plausible by Tennyson's confession that he loved 'the graceful tact, the Christian art' all the more because they were Hallam's, and that it was love for his friend that spurred on his 'imitative will' to emulate the virtues his life exhibited: as if *In Memoriam* were written as a *De Imitatione Hallami*. In lyric CXII the Hallam-Christ parallel is repeated, as Hallam is imaged as one who

> ... tracts of calm from tempests made.   (CXII)

with a recollection of Christ calming the storm (Matt. 8:23-27). No wonder that Tennyson says that his friend fills 'all the room / Of all my love' (CXII). [1]

---

[1] Thomas Carlyle, *Sartor Resartus*, in the Centenary Edition, edited by H. D. Traill, 30 vols. (1896-1901), I, 54. For John Tyndall, see Tess Cosslett, *The 'Scientific Movement' and Victorian Literature*, especially Chapter 1, 'The Values of Science'.

The account of Hallam as one whose hand a child would take unasked recalls images used elsewhere in the poem. In LIV Tennyson describes himself as a 'child crying in the night', and in CXIV as a 'child in doubt and fear' who cries knowing his father will be nearby. In answer to the child's cry

> Out of darkness [come] the hands
>
> That reach thro' nature, moulding man . (CXXIV)

In lyric LXXXIV earlier, Tennyson had dreamed of the 'shining hand' of Christ reaching out to take both him and Hallam together, only to reject the dream as a reed to lean on, merely disrupting the 'low beginnings of content'. But from the first lyric onwards Tennyson has reached out his hands: to catch 'the far-off interest of tears' in I, towards the 'empty hands' of Nature in III, 'lame hands of faith' that seize only the chaff in LV. In XIV he had imagined how it would be if Hallam were not dead after all, and

> The man I held as half-divine
>
> Should strike a sudden hand in mine, (XIV)

But the hands that have reached him were indeed Hallam's, in the trance of XCV, when 'The dead man touch'd me from the past'. In lyric LXXX Tennyson reflects that if he had died before Hallam, his friend would have been able to turn loss and sorrow into gain:

> His credit thus shall set me free. (XXX)

We can hardly miss the Christian ransom imagery here. Hallam's influence will be to Tennyson an 'example from the grave', which will

> Reach out dead hands to comfort me. (LXXX)

Tennyson has reached out a hand; what it clasps is the hand of Hallam.

The last group of Christmas poems provides a further, almost shocking illustration of the way Hallam comes to usurp the place of Christ in the poem. In lyric CV Tennyson writes of the family's decision to abandon the traditional Christmas festivities after they had moved away from the house at Somersby where the traditions had grown up:

> For who would keep an ancient form
>
> Thro' which the spirit breathes no more? (CV)

The following poem rings out the old year and rings in the new:

> Ring in the valiant man and free,
>
> > The larger heart, the kindlier hand ...
>
> Ring in the Christ that is to be. (CVI)

There can be little doubt whose has been 'the kindlier hand' in this poem, and the next lyric is indeed a celebration, not of Christ's birthday, but of Hallam's: 'We keep the day' (CVII).

Tennyson himself may have been unsure about some of the implications of *In Memoriam*. He revised it assiduously over the years, but by far the most significant change was not made until 1872. Originally lyric XCV had read

> *His* living soul was flash'd on mine.

This was altered in the 1872 edition to '*The* living soul...'. The substitution of the article for the pronoun clearly reduces (though it does not exclude) the suggestion in the earlier version that Tennyson had been in direct personal contact with Hallam. It also opens up a possible allusion to Wordsworth's account in 'Tintern Abbey' of how 'we are laid asleep / In body, and become a living soul' (11.46-7), which takes us still further away from Tennyson's immediate experience in the garden at Somersby. This is in keeping with his later comments on the poem, which emphasise its representative rather than its personal character: 'It must be remembered that this is a poem, *not* an actual biography ... "I" in the poem is not always the author speaking of himself, but the voice of the human race speaking through him.' To point to this distancing of himself from the poem is not to accuse Tennyson of dishonesty: no doubt as the years passed he felt the need to revise his understanding of the trance described in XCV. It is however to suggest that *In Memoriam* reveals more of itself, is all the more moving, if we see it as an essentially personal poem, only in part to be brought within the bounds of orthodoxy. We shall appreciate it most, I suggest, if we see in it, as George Eliot did, 'the sanctification of human love as religion'.[1]

---

[8] *Alfred Lord Tennyson: A Memoir*, I, 304-5. For George Eliot's comments, originally made in the *Westminster Review* in October 1855, see *Essays of George Eliot*, edited by T. Pinney (1963), p. 191. After the death of G. H. Lewes in 1878 George Eliot copied sections of *In Memoriam* into her diary.

III Thomas Hardy's Attitude towards Christianity

– P. W. Coxon

Unlike his friend and close contemporary Edmund Gosse, who successfully expunged from his voluminous <u>oeuvre</u> the traces of his religious upbringing in a home dedicated to a puritanical brand of biblical fundamentalism (his parents were devout members of the Exclusive Brethren), Thomas Hardy's early association with the established Church was a happy one. Indeed, from the perspective of old age it is looked back on with a degree of nostalgic affection. His novels and poetry testify to the formative influence of the Church, the Bible and the Prayer Book on his creative imagination. From the earliest fictional prose of *Under the Greenwood Tree* which lovingly evokes the musical activities of the village choir of a previous generation and the sharp theological debate on the practice of infant baptism in *The Laodicean,* to the poignant depiction of Tess's dilemma over the baptism and burial of her child Sorrow in *Tess of the d'Urbevilles,* and Jude's fascination for biblical studies and a clerical destiny via the dreaming spires of Oxford in *Jude the Obscure,* the novelist's brooding thoughts are never far from the core institution of his native heath: the Church of England and its moral imperatives. The preoccupation is constant but the attitude shifts and changes simply because Hardy himself whilst still in his twenties became a reluctant agnostic. In *Thomas Hardy: Distracted Preacher?* (1989) T.Hands has argued cogently that the two major movements which chartered Church life during Hardy's formative years, Evangelicalism and Tractarianism, are consummately worked into the fabric of the two major achievements which marked his career as a novelist, *Tess* and *Jude*, the one exorcising his Evangelical past, the other his High Church past.[1]   The fact that Hardy had been described as a 'Christian at heart',[2]   *Tess* 'one of the most profoundly Christian novels in the whole of English literature'[3]   and that a 'churchy' man was Hardy's description of himself [4] suggest a rich complexity of ideology in this area only too facilely resolved by the equation that Hardy believed in his heart but did not believe in his head.

A man's relationship to his God, as H. Orel puts it, however much he may regard it as his own business, invites investigation if it becomes the subject matter of his

---

[1] Pp. 71-75, 111-114

[2] F.B. Pinion, *A Hardy Companion. A Guide to the Works of Thomas Hardy and their Background* (1968), p.167.

[3] A bishop's description of the novel recorded in Rosemary Harthill's exploration of the relationship between God and the poets on BBC Radio Three in March, 1992.

[4] *The Life and Work of Thomas Hardy*, ed. by M. Millgate (1984), p.407.

art.[1] The heavy freight of transferred autobiography in much of Hardy's verse - what he called the personal particulars of his life - is self-evident. Hardy himself claimed that there were more details of his life and thought in his verse than in the novels and he also believed that he would be left alone to express freely what he felt without the critics scalding his neck. Distressed by the abuse which followed the publication of *Jude*, but financially secure, he turned back to what had always been his first love. He had every hope of pursuing the poetic vocation free from the strife that marked his career as a novelist and of being left alone to express his true feelings:

> Perhaps I can express more fully in verse ideas and emotions which run counter to the inert chrystallized opinion...which the vast body of men have vested interests in supporting. To cry out in a passionate poem that (for instance) the Supreme Mover or Movers, the Prime Force or Forces, must be either limited in power, unknowing, or cruel - which is obvious enough, and has been for centuries - will cause them merely a shake of the head; but to put it in argumentative prose will make them sneer, or foam, and set all the literary contortionists jumping upon me, a harmless agnostic, as if I were a clamorous atheist, which in their crass illiteracy they seem to think is the same thing...If Galileo had said in verse that the world moved, the Inquisition might have let him alone. [2]

In the years following Hardy published as many as a thousand poems in eight volumes of verse ranging from *Wessex Poems* in 1898 to *Winter Words*, his last collection, prepared by himself but appearing shortly after his death in 1928. Many of these are associated with religion and the incessant conflict between faith and doubt. They range from poignant memories of a childhood unclouded by the increasing <u>Angst</u> of the Victorian age when the juvenile Hardy attended the parish church, took part in its services, sang hymns and psalms, absorbed the resonances of the Authorised Version, recollected the activities of his father's band and delighted in the vagaries of clergymen. Some touched on the challenges of the modern biblical criticism and the threat posed for religious belief; others dealt with the yearning obsession with death. Taking the spiritual baton from Job, Hardy also struggled with the problem of theodicy: how could a loving and all-powerful God allow undeserved pain and injustice in the world? One curious poem eschews any attempt to define the basis of Christian faith but surmises that maybe God has forgotten the world he created so long ago. In *God-Forgotten* the poet, like Daniel in the Old Testament, takes on the role of an apocalyptic visionary and gains

---

[5] H. Orel, *The Final Years of Thomas Hardy: 1922-1928* (1976), p.108. I am deeply indebted to Orel's seminal study of Hardy's views on Christianity in ch.7 of this book and in particular his choice of poems and judicious comments on them.

[6] *The Life*, p.302

admittance to the presence of the Ancient of Days to regale Him with an account of the earth's suffering. The stilted parlance and eccentricity of the Creator combine to imply that man is not solely responsible for the state of things below:

-'The Earth, sayest thou? The Human race?
By Me created? Sad its lot?
Nay: I have no remembrance of such place:
 Such world I fashioned not'.-

 -'O Lord, forgive me when I say
  Thou spakest the word that made it all'.-
'The Earth of men - let me bethink me...Yea!
  I dimly do recall

'Some tiny sphere I built long back...

'It lost my interest from the first,
 My aims therefore succeeding ill
Haply it died of doing as it durst?'-
  'Lord, it existeth still'.-

The idea that God shared some responsibility for what happened subsequent to the creation is echoed in Edward Fitzgerald's rendering of the *Rubaiyat 58* recited to Hardy by request as he lay dying at Max Gate:

Oh, Thou, who Man of baser Earth didst make,
And who with Eden didst devise the Snake;
For all the Sin wherewith the Face of Man
Is blacken'd, Man's Forgiveness give - and take!

In Hardy's fantasy, when God realizes that the 'tainted ball' exists and suffers, Messengers are sent

...and straightway put an end
To what men undergo...

The sentiments of this poem alone would have been enough, he thought, to jeopardise any chance he might have had of becoming Poet Laureate (Robert Bridges filled the vacancy following the death of Alfred Austin in 1913). Trawling through the poems more themes emerge, including fascination with early dogma (Hardy recalled in *The Life* that the dogmatic superstitions read every Sunday in church were 'merely a commemorative recitation of old articles of faith held by our grandfathers'[1]), thorough scrutiny and questioning of the value of the Christian religion, man's brutish behaviour in the modern world despite the example of Jesus, and an increasingly sombre mood and feeling of hopelessness generated by the horrors of the First World War.

Hardy had long been interested in the religious potential of the established Church stripped of what he called 'theological lumber'. Writing to his friend Edward Clodd in 1902 he expanded on the efforts of humanists and rationalists to shake it off:

> If the doctrines of the supernatural were quietly abandoned tomorrow by the Church, and 'reverence and love for an ethical ideal' alone retained, not one in ten thousand would object to the readjustment, whilst the enormous bulk of thinkers excluded by the old teaching would be brought into the fold, and our venerable old churches and cathedrals would become the centres of emotional life that they once were.[2]

In the *Apology* to *Late Lyrics and Earlier* published twenty years later he still had hopes that the 'hesitating English instinct towards liturgical restatement' would be overcome and the new Prayer Book would finally have its liturgy recast at the expense of the old supernatural elements, thereby 'gathering...many millions of waiting agnostics into the fold.'[3] To the end of his life Hardy maintained a personal affection for Anglican traditions; writing to John Morley in 1885 he revelled in the prospect that one day the structure of the Church would be modified and ethically regenerated:

> I have sometimes had a dream that the church, instead of being disendowed, could be made to modulate by degrees (say as the present incumbents die out) into an undogmatic, non-theological establishment for the promotion of virtuous living on which all honest men are agreed - leaving to voluntary bodies the organization of whatever societies they may think best for teaching their various forms of doctrinal religion.[4]

The charge that he was an anti-Christian libertine (in the manner, say, of Zola) hurt him deeply and often he felt the need to lay out his programme clearly to unbiased readers. His apologies for his work were forthright and clear:

> To exhibit what I feel ought to be exhibited about life, to show that what we call immorality, in religion etc. are often true morality, true religion etc. quite freely to the end.[5]

---

[1] ibid, p. 302

[2] *The Collected Letters of Thomas Hardy*, vol.III: 1902-1908, edited by R.L.Purdy and M. Millgate, p.5. Printed in seven volumes, Hardy's letters cited hereafter as CL.

[3] *Thomas Hardy's Personal Writings* (1966), ed. H. Orel, p.57.

[4] CL I, p. 136

[5] ibid, IV, p. 28

However, he knew of no other 'purely English establishment' that had comparable 'dignity and footing, with such strength and association, such scope for transmutability, such architectural spell' like that of the Church, that could 'keep the shreds of morality together'.[1] The 'shreds of morality' were of great concern to Victorian writers, especially perhaps to those who had relinquished their Christian beliefs. F.W.H. Myers re-called the 'terrible earnestness' of George Eliot as he strolled with her in the Fellows' garden of Trinity College, Cambridge, in May 1873. Taking as her cue the three words <u>God</u>, <u>Immortality</u> and <u>Duty</u>, she expostulated 'how inconceivable was the first, how unbelievable was the second, and how peremptory and absolute the third...'. Nietzsche, as Professor Furness has recently reminded us, poured scorn on Eliot's retention of absolute standards of morality, her 'flabby humanism' as he put it.[2] Hardy had been called many things by various critics. He lists them ('Nonconformist, Agnostic, Atheist, Infidel, Immoralist, Heretic, Pessimist or something else equally opprobrious... '[3]) and expresses surprise that his instinctively religious nature had never been pinpointed. More plausibly they might as well have called him

> churchy; not in an intellectual sense, but insofar as instincts and emotions ruled. As a child, to be a parson had been his dream; moreover he had had several clerical relatives who held livings; while his grandfather, uncle, brother, wife, cousin, and two sisters had been musicians in various churches over a period covering altogether more than a hundred years. He himself had frequently read the church lessons, and had at one time as a young man begun reading for Cambridge with a view to taking Orders.[4]

The new edition of the Prayer Book in the mid-twenties was in the event, a profound disappointment to Hardy. The bishops had not dropped the 'preternatural assumptions' from the liturgy and henceforth he 'lost all expectation of seeing the Church representative of modern thinking minds'.[5] The 'architectural spell' of the Church was a different matter. The potentialities of architecture had served as a source of moral and social criteria throughout the novels as Millgate has pointed out,[6] and the same may be claimed for many of the poems. In *Far from the Madding Crowd* the church comes off second best to the barn in usefulness to the farming community in much the same way as in *The Laodicean* Stancy Castle, linked with the outmoded mediaevalism of the Church's teaching, is contrasted to the buzzing telephone wire, token of the 'fever and fret' of modern times. And in *Jude*, the

---

[1] *Apology to Late Lyrics and Earlier* (1922); see also, *Personal Writings*, p.57.

[2] See p. 10 supra.

[3] *The Life*, p. 407

[4] ibid., pp. 407 and 465

[5] ibid., p. 448

[6] In *Thomas Hardy: His Career as a Novelist* (1971) , p. 170 (hereafter Career)

young stonemason, planning a tryst with his girlfriend in the cathedral, is told in no uncertain terms that the cathedral has had its day and she would prefer to meeting in the railway station. 'Architectural spell' is not to be construed as a simple question of admiration for gothic architecture but betokens the ambiguity and complexity of Hardy's attitude to the Church, the tender memories of past associations jolting against the force of superceding structures based on rational necessity.

At the age of twenty-two Hardy left home for London with two letters of introduction for prospective employers, a return railway ticket in his pocket, and for spiritual fare his Bible and Prayer Book. From marginal notes in his devotional books it appears that the young Hardy, whose Church attendance and devotional practice were largely instinctive and harmonized by family practice adhered basically to Anglican principles, and had at the age of twenty even made some sort of commitment to Christ. It was during the London period that his opinions changed radically. Not only does his church attendance decline - this can be gauged from the decreasing number of dated annotations in his Bible and Prayer Book - but, as Hands has pointed out,[1] a completely alien note is sounded. In 1864 the single word 'doubt' with the date (11 September) was pencilled in against the text in Isaiah 45 which reads 'I am God and there is none else.'[2] The Judaic claim of exclusive monotheism, taken over in toto into Christian theology, is challenged by Hardy and marks the commencement of his pilgrimage of unbelief. The poems discussed here chart Hardy's contribution to the store of great nineteenth century poetry which was concerned with the loss of faith in a brave new world

> ...which seems
> To lie before us like a land of dreams,
> So various, so beautiful, so new,

but which

> Hath really neither joy, nor love, nor light,
> Nor certitude, nor peace, nor help for pain...[3]

---

[1] Hands, p. 30

[2] According to Hands, the word was subsequently erased. It was only revealed with the aid of specialized infra-red photographic equipment.

[3] Dover Beach (1867).

Repudiation of the supernatual was one of the cardinal tenets of writers like Matthew Arnold, who had rejected conventional Christian belief with its insistence on the literal authority of scripture. Hardy picked up the theme in a number of his poems, none more forcefully than in the long poem *Panthera* which implicitly denies the virgin birth, drawing on the legend of a Roman centurion who believes that the figure on Calvary is the son he fathered three decades earlier in Nazareth. Drawing on material culled from D. Strauss' *Das Leben Jesu* and E. Haeckel's *Die Welträtsel*, Hardy tried to demythologise the Christ of the New Testament and adumbrate the true achievements of the historical Jesus, the object of the exercise being to preserve a rationally plausible basis for an up-to-date Christian religion. In the *Apology* to *Late Lyrics and Earlier*[1] Hardy expressed the hope for 'an alliance between religion, which must be retained unless the world is to perish, and complete rationality, which must come, unless also the world is to perish'.[2] He looked upon the virgin birth as a beautiful myth, but so irrational that perhaps it kept many from appreciating Jesus for his teachings. Arnold thought that Christians should ignore supersititions that obscured the true greatness of Jesus, his 'sweet reasonableness' and message to the world. One of the most striking poems of *Winter Words*, <u>An Evening in Galilee</u> closes with Mary looking pensively towards Jezreel, possibly a catchword linking the poem with *Panthera* - it was from this direction that the centurion, the father of her child, had come so many years ago. In the form of a soliloquy Mary finds no solace for the 'tragedy brink' of her son's career by regarding him as one of the ecstatic prophets; rather she wonders if he has lost his wits and describes what he professes as 'far too grotesque to be true'. The awful sonority of her son's rejection of her (he asks 'Who is my mother?') is cleverly inverted by her rejoinder: he might advisedly have asked 'who is my father?' '<u>That</u> no one knows but Joseph and - one other...' she confesses. Her concerns are of the earth, earthly and set the historical Jesus within the parameters of credible if unconventional humanity. A conventional mother figure herself, Mary is concerned about his bohemian dress, the sort of people he is mixed up with, and the threat to his reputation by a 'woman of no good character'. Her son is a preacher and expositor and in her eyes is no fabulous miracle-worker. J.O. Bailey argues that in centering Mary's thought upon Jesus' madness, Hardy intended an ironic contrast to the Arnoldian sweet reasonableness of Jesus' message.[3] More importantly, however, 'she is wholly human and she thinks of Jesus as explainable, for all his unconventional behaviour, without recourse to the imagery of supernatural agencies'.[4] Stanley Spencer-like is the juxtaposition of the poem with <u>Henley</u>

---

[1] Hardy's sixth volume of verse published in 1922.

[2] *Personal Writings,* p. 57

[3] In *The Poetry of Thomas Hardy: A Handbook and Commentary* (1970), p.599.

[4] Orel, p.110.

Regatta in the *Winter Words* volume: Hardy was not averse to shocking contemporary readers with his realism.

Hardy's attitude to the miraculous in Christian tradition is again finely caught in the poem In the Servants' Quarters which treats the account of Peter's denial of Christ with imaginative realism. As in Evening in Galilee Hardy picks details from the Synoptic gospels (and from John) to piece together an impressively realistic account of Jesus' arraignment prior to trial and execution in terms of the arrest, interrogation and torture of any dangerous felon. One edition of the poem, read on record by Richard Burton, superbly evokes its down to earth thrust: Peter responds to the awkward questions in a Scottish accent. The unfriendly barmaid and the streetwise constables immediately identify his provincial northern origin ('Why, man, you speak the dialect/He uses in his answers; you can hear him up the stairs'). The supernatural would be out of place here. Bailey observes that 'Hardy simply treated the episode realistically' as Browning, among other Victorian writers, had done in depicting similar biblical scenes.[1] The rhetorical question 'And he is risen?' in A Drizzling Easter Morning which forms an inclusio with the final statement 'though risen is he' in the last line of the poem, suggests an ambivalent mixture of willingness to believe and disbelief. There are two voices in the poem, positive and negative, and its structure mandates choice, whatever one's personal interpretive predisposition may be. On the one hand, the weary wain plodding forward and the dead men in the graveyard become significant for the whole experience of suffering and evil. On the other hand, without belief it is only another rainy morning in March or April and for the poet in the rain no less than for those who are already in the grave, it makes no difference given that Jesus is risen: the old pattern of work continues regardless of the resurrection event in much the same way as in Brueghel's famous painting The Fall of Icarus 'everything turns away' when the young man plunges to his death - the ploughman keeps resolutely to his furrow, the shepherd star-gazes and the 'expensive delicate ship', as Auden puts it, sails calmly on.[2] In the fine late poem Drinking Song Hardy 'sets the substance of a university lecture to the rollicking rhythm of a student-chorus in a beer-hall'.[3] The historical development of civilization revolves on a series of speculations or philosophies on the nature of human existence by such worthies as Thales, Copernicus, Hume, Darwin, Cheyne and Einstein, none of which offered a

---

[1] Bailey, p. 329

[2] In his poem Musée des Beaux Arts which is a fine poetic response to the painting.

[3] Bailey, p.614. Hands has drawn attention to numerous illustrations in the novels where Hardy "instead of attempting to show drink and religion as adversaries and opposites...delights in documenting their close association"(pp.93f.).

definitive solution to the riddle of existence but each of which was in vogue for a season. T.K. Cheyne, Oriel Professor of the Interpretation of Scripture at Oxford University, seems to be the odd man out in this illustrious pantheon but Hardy has included him as the articulate iconoclast of the miraculous element in Christianity. Among other things he laid to rest the received tradition of the virgin birth.[1] 'Such tale, indeed', Cheyne retorts in his capacity as a biblical scholar, 'helps not our creed', and is 'a tale long known to none'. The pessimism of the poem is however relieved in the climax of the final refrain of the chorus:

> We'll do a good deed nevertheless!

Hardy's readiness to venture into historical and literary criticism of the Bible was evident in *Panthera*. A delightful satire on the dire effects of Higher Criticism appears in the single rhyming *The Respectable Burgher* which actually has the subtitle <u>On "The Higher Criticism"</u>. Although the poem appears first in *Poems of the Past and Present* (1901) it is regarded as much older and according to Edmund Blunden was composed in response to the publication in 1860 of *Essays and Reviews*, a book which he associates with the mental coming of age of the young Thomas Hardy. This famous collection was denounced by many clergymen even more clamorously, and accused of undermining faith in the Bible more treacherously than Darwin's *On the Origin of Species by Means of Natural Selection* which had appeared a year earlier. Such was the outcry against it that its authors, the 'Reverend Doctors' of Hardy's poem, were dubbed 'The Seven against Christ'.[2] Hardy was amused to think that many a respectable citizen would find Voltaire's scepticism "moderate" compared to the Higher Criticism, which began with German scholars who analysed the biblical records from a scientific and historical angle. Fourteen years earlier, in fact, George Eliot had translated Strauss' *Das Leben Jesu* and her contempt for the blinkered vision of the established Church in the face of modern thinking is reflected in the portrayal of Casaubon that 'scholarly clergyman and creditable to the cloth' who married Dorothea in her novel *Middlemarch* (published in instalments in 1871-1872). Engaged on his monumental *A Key to all Mythologies*, he is criticised by the young radical Will Ladislaw who remarks that 'if Casaubon read German he would save himself a great deal of trouble' because 'the Germans have taken the lead in historical inquiries...and laugh at results which are got by groping about in woods with a pocket compass while they have made good roads'! Bailey suggests that Hardy joins hands here with Matthew Arnold in entertaining

---

[1] Or did he? In an interview entitled Heretic and Holy Man which appeared in the April 1992 edition of Alpha magazine "the unbelieving bishop", as the editor, David Roberts, called the Bishop of Durham, Dr. David Jenkins, endorsed the view that the virgin birth and the resurrection were not historical events. Asked if the body of Jesus could still be discovered in a Middle Eastern tomb, the bishop replied, "I think so". And asked if he believed Jesus was born "without the seed of an earthly father", the bishop replied: "No". Panthera *redidivus*?

[2] *The Life*, p.37.

misgivings about the development of biblical criticism: Hardy accepted Arnold's position that the Bible be regarded as a poetic record of religious experience and be retained as an ethical guide.[1]   According to this view *The Respectable Burgher* 'satirizes the Higher Criticism as Arnold did, for its misleading excesses'. It seems to me that Bailey is confusing the voice of the Burgher for the voice of Hardy; the poet's double-edged satire on Higher Criticism represents the response of a matter-of-fact citizen of the middle class who is sent off in alarm to 'read that modern man Voltaire'. Hardy never ceased to be fascinated by the literary complexity of biblical narrative, which he feared had been lost sight of in the pursuit of narrow historicism. In 1906 he recalled a discussion with Leslie Stephen way back in 1874 when *Far from the Madding Crowd* was being serialized in *The Cornhill Magazine*:

> Somehow we launched upon the subject of David and Saul...I spoke to the effect that the Bible account would take a good deal of beating, and that I wondered why the clergy did not argue the necessity of plenary inspiration from the marvellous artistic cunning with which so many Bible personages, like those of Saul and David, were developed...Stephen, who had been silent, then said, Yes but they never do the obvious thing; presently adding in a dry grim tone, If you wish to get an idea of Saul and David you should study them as presented by Voltaire in his drama...[2]

The secular, non-allegorical origin of <u>The Song of Songs</u> which celebrates 'the fleshly Fair' in *The Respectable Burgher* is another example of the extent of Hardy's critical reading. He multiplies illustrations of biblical lore newly thrown open to question. The last straw is doubt over the resurrection and at this point the burgher reaches his decision:

> Since thus they hint, nor turn a hair,
>   All churchgoing will I forswear,
>   And sit on Sundays in my chair,
> And read that moderate main Voltaire.

The <u>Song of Songs</u> criticism crops up in *Jude,* Hardy's last major novel: Sue Brideshead, fresh from Training College, pours scorn on Jude Fawley's theological texts which promoted the traditional allegorical interpretation:

> And what a literary enormity this is, she said, as she glanced into the pages of Solomon's Song. I mean the synopsis at the head of each   chapter, explaining away the real nature of that rhapsody. You needn't be alarmed; nobody claims inspiration for the Chapter headings... Jude looked pained. You are quite Voltairean! he murmured.[3]

---

[1]   Bailey, p.175

[2]   F.W. Maitland, *The Life and Letters of Leslie Stephen* (1906), p.274.

[3] *Jude*, Part Third, ch. iv.

Religion was never rejected outright by Hardy. He respected the Arnoldian dictum that poetry and religion were contiguous, or rather modulated each other, i.e. religion 'in its essential and undogmatic sense.'[1] What he looked for was an alliance between religion which 'must be retained unless the world is to perish' and rationality which could be achieved by means of the 'interfusing effects of poetry'.[2] Hardy reacted strongly against the dogma and doctrinal beliefs of the age which seemed to him to pale in the face of historical, geological, linguistic and other evidence. He also feared that the simplicity of the faith of Jesus had become distorted and transformed into something far removed from its pristine source. The modern church had moved away from the plain vision of its founder and had become caught in the trammels of Pauline dogma. In St Paul's a While Ago the apostle Paul is portrayed as 'that strange Jew, Damascus-bound', with a 'vision-seeing mind/ Charmless, blank in every kind' whose gesticulations and 'eager stammering speech' on the cathedral steps would have conveyed to passers-by little more than the expressions of 'an epilept enthusiast'. Paul's ecstatic vision with its emphasis on the primacy of faith over good works, sin and penance over against Jesus' message of neighbourly kindness and forgiveness is fittingly imaged in the drifts of gray illumination which spill down from the high windows of the cathedral. The 'sweet reasonableness' of Jesus and the joy of living are squeezed out here. Antipathy to Paul, the primary exemplar of dogma, recurs in Hardy's fiction, and it is hardly surprising that the religious establishment of the late nineteenth century took offence at the way it found expression in his novels. When Alec d'Urbeville becomes an itinerant preacher Tess hears him preaching a sermon 'as might be expected...of the extremist antinomian type; on justification by faith, as expounded in the theology of St Paul'. Astounded by this 'ghastly *bizarrerie*', Tess notes Alec's transfiguration from 'Paganism' to 'Paulinism'. In *The Return of the Native* Clym Yeobright quotes from St Paul to explain his leaving the diamond trade and to Eustacia he is actually reminiscent of the Apostle Paul. The self-denial determined by John Loveday in *The Trumpet Major* - 'that men of the military ought not to be like St Paul, I mean' - again reflects the influence of the apostle's 'charmless mind'. And Millgate points out that in *Tess* Angel 'affects to have revolted against the Paulinism of his temperament and upbringing, but at the crisis of relationship with Tess he proves to be still its slave'.[3] Again, Paul's attitude is reflected in the disposition of Angel's father, old Mr Clare, who 'loved Paul of Tarsus, liked St John, hated St James as much as he dared and regarded with mixed feelings Timothy, Titus and Philemon. The New Testament was less a Christiad than a

---

[1] *Personal Writings*, p. 56

[2] ibid. p. 17.

[3] *Career*, p. 275

Pauliad to his intelligence - less an argument than an intoxication'.[1]   In January
1897 Hardy confessed to E. Clodd:
> The older one gets the more deplorable seems the effect of that terrible,
> dogmatic ecclesiasticism Christianity - so-called (but really Paulinism plus
> idolatry) - on morals and true religion: a dogma with which the real teaching
> of Christ has hardly anything in common.[2]

Jesus had introduced a message of love and 'Christian' virtue; Paul had come along
and made a mess of it. The antithesis between his and Paul's teaching similarly
stimulated the imagination of Gide in *La Symphonie Pastorale* (1919). The
clergyman narrator of the story believed that 'many of the notions that constitute our
Christian faith originate not from Christ's own words but from Paul's commentaries'.
Faced with the choice of Christ and Paul in his education programme for Gertrude
he chose Christ, with disastrous consequences.[3]

The technique of ironic contrast which Hardy uses to effect in the St Paul's poem
(Paul's intoxicated visions and the interests of the modern period as exemplified in
the cadaverous statues among which visitors loiter combine to dispel Christian joy)
reappears in Winter Night in Woodland, first published in *Country Life* in 1924.
The last stanza presents the message of Christ's birth carried from house to house
by the carol-singers of the Mellstock choir ('...afoot on their yearly rounds,/ To
rouse by worn carols each house in their bounds...') which contrasts with the bunch
of smugglers, poachers, drunks and fox-hunters who carry on regardless of Robert
Penny, the Dewys, Mail and Voss who stand for the piety of an age lost and gone.
The poem discloses memories of Hardy's ancestors and the activities of the choir
that operated before he was born and which he immortalized in *Under the
Greenwood Tree* (1872). The 'rhythm of voices and strings' which waft the 'worn
carols' of the gospel through the midnight air 'From dim distance' does not mitigate
the savagery and violence of men's behaviour.

In the last poem published in his lifetime Hardy continued to explore the idea that
the lot of mankind had not been hugely improved by Christ's having lived and died.[4]
If in *Winter Night* he juxtaposed tableaux of Christian piety and man's brutality, in
Christmas in the Elgin Room he sets the pagan past in opposition to the Christian
present. The poem presents a phantasy in which the Elgin marbles, representing the

---

[1] *Tess*, Phase the Fourth, ch. XXVV

[2] *CL* II, p. 143

[3] Kipling, too, used a similar dichotomy of attitudes to great effect in his short story *The Church that was at
Antioch* in which "Paul is eclipsed as a figure of authority by Peter"; see Phillip Mallett(ed.), *Rudyard Kipling:
Limits and Renewals* (Penguin Classics, 1987), p.22.

[4] See Orel, p.112.

Greek gods, exchange views on what the peal of Christmas bells means. Christ's birth which the occasion celebrates was said, according to the Marbles

> ...to have been a day of cheer,
> And source of grace
> To the human race
> Long ere their woven sails
> winged us to exile here.

They missed the sun of their homeland and protested vigorously at their forced removal and exile to the gloom of a northern land and 'this gaunt room which sunlight shuns...'. They could only sigh for the halcyon days 'before this Christ was known, and we had good men's will. Hardy is not indulging here in facile qualitative comparisons between the fair deities sculpted by Pheidias and the Christian Deity and Christian values. He is aware that Demeter, Persephone and old Helios belong to the radiant past but he finds it difficult to discern much that is joyous here and now despite the clanging of the church bells. The Marbles in exile are not assured that the warm light of Christ any more than sweet Aurore can break through to their chill mausoleum. Their's is the confession of Swinburne's <u>Hymn to Proserpine</u>:

> Thou has conquered, O Pale Galilean; the world
> has grown grey from thy breath;
> We have drunken of things Lethean, and fed on the
> fulness of death.

The celebrated Arnoldian opposition between Judaism and Hellenism is well caught in Hardy's poem and parallels the critical perspective to Christian culture in the later novels.[1] One is reminded of the Classical statuettes Sue placed on her chest of drawers and addressed with passages from Gibbon and Swinburne (including the <u>Proserpine</u> lines).

Hardy was chary of greeting the advances of civilization enthusiastically. During the course of the Boer War he wrote to his friend, Florence Henniker:
> I met a religious man on Friday...and I said, We the civilized world, have given Christianity a fair trial for nearly 2000 years, and it has not yet taught countries the rudimentary virtue of keeping peace: so why not throw it over and try, say Buddhism?...It shocked him, for he could only see the unchristianity of Kruger.[2]

---

[1] See Hands p. 904.

[2] *CL*, p. 248.

After the First World War these sentiments were galvanized in the blistering quatrain <u>Christmas</u>: <u>1924</u>:

> 'Peace upon earth!' was said, We sing it,
> And pay a million priests to bring it,
> After two thousand years of mass
> We've got as far as poison-gas.

Orel finds it 'difficult to tell if Hardy laments here the tattering of the dreams of the League of Nations more or less than he laments the futility of the message preached by "a million priests", the invocation of "Peace upon earth!" which apparently means little or nothing to the modern world'.[1] The brutality of the war horrified him and he regretted the optimistic note which marked the epilogue of his great epic <u>The Dynasts</u>. Millgate nevertheless presses for a more moderate assessment:

> Fundamentally pessimistic about the human condition in the sense that he believed birth and coming to consciousness to be a kind of original doom, Hardy could nevertheless respond with compassion to human and (animal) suffering and bring a reformist zeal to bear upon evils perceived as social and hence as potentially susceptible to amelioration or even eradication. He could also remain perpetually alert to the possibility, however, faint, of some 'blessed hope' of which the most diligent search had thus far left him 'unaware'...[2]

Millgate alludes here to one of the finest poems in the Hardy canon, <u>The Darkling Thrush</u>. From dazzling images which build up a picture of death and desolation the voice of the thrush takes up such an evensong of joy

> That I could think there trembled through
> > His happy good-night air
> Some blessed Hope, whereof he knew
> > And I was unaware.

In a number of poems Hardy achieves a teasing balance between knowing and unknowing, perception and imperception, belief and disbelief - what he conjoins as 'the gleam and gloom' in the provocative poem <u>God's Funeral</u>. <u>The Oxen,</u> for example, is a fine example of Hardy's nostalgia for the firm faith of his childhood ('Nor did it occur to one of us there/To doubt...') which jostled uncomfortably with the perceived truths of adulthood ('So fair a fancy few would weave/In these years!') - he longs to recapture the faith of his Victorian childhood, but is unable to

---

[43] Orel, p. 113

[44] M. Millgate, *Thomas Hardy: A Bibliography* (1982), pp.410-411.

do so. In a recent B.B.C. broadcast Rosemary Harthill suggested that in the gloom Hardy has identified his own religious epitaph: 'Hoping it might be so'. Indeed the pastoral and spiritual nature of the poem, including the hope heralded in the last stanza ('I should go with him in the gloom,/Hoping it might be so'), has not discouraged its absorption into modern Christmas anthologies; set to music, for instance, it was the first carol sung in King's College, Cambridge at a recent traditional Christmas Eve recital.[1] Donald Davie, however, excluded it from *The New Oxford Book of Christian Verse* (1981) on the grounds that it belonged to 'that special class of agnostic and very moving poems' - Philip Larkin's <u>Church Going</u> is another example - 'that wish to believe, though they cannot'.[2] Perhaps this judgement puts too low a premium on hope as one of the principles of Christian ethics. Tennyson's *In Memoriam* certainly presents Christian doubt in a positive light. 'And faintly trust the larger hope' is the memorable last line of section LV in a poem often weak on faith, and full of doubt. As section XCVI has it

> There lives more faith in honest doubt,
> Believe me, than in half the creeds.

But the poem is also strong on hope:

> Oh yet we trust that somehow good
> Will be the final goal of ill...(LIV)

Some of the best poetry of the nineteenth century is concerned with the loss of faith,[3] and Hardy, acquainted with *In Memoriam* from his early teens, was certainly aware of the issue very early in his life. Tennyson somehow found a way to assuage his doubts and remain a Christian, unlike Hardy whose poetry witnesses to the titanic struggle waged in his mind betwen faith and doubt. In his great poem Tennyson gave voice to the Victorian crisis of confidence in the Christian credo

> Are God and nature then at strife
> That nature lends such evil dreams?
> So careful of the type she seems,
> So careless of the single life...
> I falter where I firmly trod (LV).

---

[1] Helen Gardner's *Faber Book of Religious Verse* adheres fairly closely to the Christian tradition although she is not averse to errant masters like Shelley, Houseman and Yeats, and actually includes Hardy's <u>Darkling Thrush </u>in her collection.

[2] P. xx

[3] See <u>supra</u> pp. 17-33

Hardy's is a bleaker vision and his emotional ambivalence, it must be said, often veers in the direction of expressions of defiance and despair, as in In Tenebris I:

> Black is night's cape;
> But death will not appal
> One who, past doubtings all,
>   Waits in unhope.

When Hardy approaches the forms of orthodox Christianity his tone gets increasingly polemical, as in the poem Unkept Good Fridays which was first published in the *Daily Telegraph* three months after his death. Again and again Hardy had argued that the distinctive morality of Christ's teachings, his humanity and altruism sat uneasily with the systematized canon of doctrines which demanded belief in the supernatural. Pinion regarded the poem as Positivist - 'in the cause of humanity Jesus was but one of many Messiahs or Redeemers':[1]

> There are many more good Fridays
> Than this, if we but knew
> The names...

Along with these other 'Christs of unwrit names' Jesus suffered in a world '...not even worthy/To taunt their hopes and aims'. The final stanza carries an unrelenting message: we have rejected the Christ we know and the nameless Christs who followed him; he and they are too good for us and we find ourselves where we are today because our Christianity is an empty stall. Orel reads the poem as a final comment on Christmas in the Elgin Room:

> The old gods are exiled, imprisoned in the British Museum, devitalised; but
> the God of Christianity, the true and living Christ, may never have been
> believed in, and...it is not in human nature, as the new Dark Age moves in
> engulfing us, to understand and appreciate the meaning of Good Friday.[2]

Hardy's disappointment with the Church of England in the mid-twenties, when the new Prayer Book appeared with a liturgy entirely unrevised with respect to rationaliistic thought, and the vastness of the gulf he saw between its institutionalized worship and the thinking man like himself who wanted to return to a simple faith, led to morose disillusionment. He acknowledged that as far as he was concerned his poems were the more individual part of his literary harvest although he disclaimed that what he called 'unadjusted impressions' contained a harmonious philosophy of life. He was perhaps too sensitive to what he took to be wilful

---

[1] F.B. Pinion, *A Commentary on the Poems of Thomas Hardy*, (1976), p. 239.

[2] Orel, p.114

misrepresentations of his voice by Grundyist reviewers, that chorus of licensed tasters he inveighed against in the introduction to his last volume of verse.[1] Even his close friend Edmund Gosse mistook his intentions and asked increduously in his review of *Jude*

> What has Providence done to Mr Hardy that he should rise up in the arable land of Wessex and shake his fist at his creator?[2]

Still, as Orel surmises,

> ...it would be strange if Hardy did not occasionally - in poems on a topic so close to his heart as the Christian faith and the difficulties he encountered as he sought to partake of its blessings - sound an unmistakable personal note.[3]

Compared to the seasonal poems already mentioned Christmastide betrays an intensely private response to the joyous season of the year. In it he draws a contrast between his mood of inner melancholy:

> The rain-shafts splintered on me
> As despondently I strode;
> The twilight gloomed upon me
> And bleared the blank high-road

and the seasonal cheer of the sodden tramp:

> A cheerful voice called, nigh me,
> A merry Christmas, friend!

Ironic contrast is also evident in another poem centred on Christmas-tide jollities, incongruously called A Nightmare, and the Next Thing. It describes the poet's early evening stroll from his home at Max Gate into downtown Dorchester on a dull, foggy Christmas day. His mood is conveyed by the description of 'the empty street...fogged and blurred' and the lampposts which, on this 'nightmare Christmas Day'

> ...just lit, begin to outloom
> Like dandelion-globes in the gloom

and is in startling juxtaposition to 'Three clammy casuals' who 'wend their way' happy ('Jimmy, this is a treat! Hay - hay!') and oblivious, like the girls in the wagonnette, unnoticing of the 'gray nightmare/Astride the day' as seen by the poet. In these verses published after Hardy's death, the poet, in contrast to the joyous

---

[1] *Winter Poems* (1928), and see Preface to *Poems of the Past and Present* (1901).

[2] Cosmopolis, Jan. 1896; p.68 (reprinted in *Thomas Hardy: The Critical Heritage* (1970) ed. R.G. Cox, p.269).

[3] Orel, pp.115-116.

salutations of his fellow-men, pours out his sorry feelings in the first person, and evinces a remarkable consistency of tone with <u>The Impercipient</u> which appeared in his first verse volume *Wessex Poems* (1898). The original title of this poem in manuscript was <u>The Agnostic</u> although it was never published as such, the change perhaps marking Hardy's spiritual odyssey from the intellectually satisfying certainties of scientific humanism and concomitant disenchantment with religion to the more complex and painful state of impercipience. Tone deaf to the music they heard and blind to the sights they saw, he simply could not feel what his believing friends felt nor embrace their beliefs . Attending service with some friends in Salisbury cathedral he lamented his sense of isolation from the 'bright believing band':

> Since heart of mine knows not that ease
> Which they know; since it be
> That He who breathes All's Well to these
> Breathes no All's-Well to me,
> My lack might move their sympathies
> And Christian charity!

Hardy uses the superb image of a bird deprived of wings - does it plummet to the earth willingly? In similar fashion his faith is not cast off deliberately or nonchalantly; he is simply deprived of the wings of faith his comrades have:

> Why always I must feel as blind
> To sights my brethren see,
> Why joys they've found I cannot find,
> Abides a mystery...
>
> Yet I would bear my shortcomings
> With meet tranquility,
> But for the charge that blessed things
> I'd liefer not have be.
> O, doth a bird deprived of wings
> Go earth-bound wilfully!

Bailey notes sensibly that the poem 'expresses his distress that both the critics, who attacked him for his unbelief, and his friends, whom his agnosticism hurt, did not see that he could not accept their new faith'.[1] To the end of his life Hardy loved church services and often attended them. He was, however, unable to supplement these activities with a theoretical undergirding consonant with his mental doubts and uncertainties.

---

[1]   Bailey, p.103.

J. Kissane emended the credal affirmation 'I think, therefore I am' to 'remember, therefore I am' to encapsulate Tennyson's passion for the past.[1] The postulate is appropriate for Hardy too, especially since in his later poems, in the dreary aftermath of the post-war years, his thoughts turned back to the certainties of his own childhood. <u>Yuletide in a Younger World</u> reflects the ageing poet's mood: in his youth he had been responsive to the

> Imminent oncomings of radiant revel -
> Doings of delight...

Phantoms, divination, small voices and even 'the far-time tones of the fire-filled prophets/Long on the earth unseen...' had caught his imagination and filled him with a sense of wonder. But the loss of faith had also sadly led to a loss of vision and made men, with whom the poet identifies, 'blinker-bound'. The serenity of yesteryear is gone for ever with no hope of reclamation: 'Can such ever have been?' he asks in the closing line of the poem. The certainties of faith which had formed the staple diet of bygone days had not been satisfyingly replaced by the victuals of scientific humanism. In <u>Afternoon Service at Mellstock</u> (<u>circa 1850)</u> Hardy recalls standing, at the age of ten, in the panelled pew of the village church

> Singing one-voiced a Tate-and-Brady psalm
> To the tune of 'Cambridge New'.

'So mindless were those outpourings', he comments,

> Though I am not aware
> That I have gained by subtle thought on things
> Since we stood psalming there.

Hands has shown on the basis of Hardy's marginal jottings that the Tate-and-Brady psalm set to 'Cambridge New' was number 78, a metrical psalm 'concerned with man's responsibility to his ancestors in handing on religious belief'.[2] As such it expresses perfectly the faith of his own ancestors which he had shared. From the historical perspective Hands finds this presentation of the Stinsford Church service 'somewhat unsatisfactorily disingenuous'[3] because the reforms initiated by Rev. Arthur Shirley indicate that Hardy's old church was in the van of tractarian reforms.

---

[1] J. Kissane, "Tennyson: The Passion for the Past and the Curse of Time",*ELH* 32 (1965), p.100.

[2] Hands, p.100.

[3] Ibid, p.10.

But surely the service remembered here is one of Hardy's great fictions. The way he recapitulated his life (as in *The Life*), his relationships and his personal particulars was very much an imaginative exercise, a construct of the mind in which memory is interfused with imagination. In <u>Afternoon Service at Mellstock</u> we impinge on the realm of impressions, not convictions, the 'question of...their consistency...being regarded as not of the first moment'.[1]   It is not the event itself but Hardy's interpretation of it that is paramount.

But what of the future, the consolation brought by descendants, the ineradicable heredity ensured by children and grandchildren? The poem <u>Heredity</u> presents the idea that the family face continues through generations

> Projecting trait and trace
> Through time to times anon,
> And leaping from place to place
> Over oblivion.

But not, it would seem, the Hardy face. His will of 1922 indicates that he had not ruled out the possibility of an heir by his second marriage, but in <u>Sine Prole</u> he expresses his final reconciliation to being childless:

> To the moment where I stand
> Has my line wound: I the last one -...
>   Of that file, so many-manned!

Hardy's conception of the barbarism of his age may have taken some consolation from the cessation of his line. He certainly articulated it to his friends, and on one occasion rather insensitively,[2] but the lines remain peculiarly poignant.

It is difficult, as Orel observed, to gauge the consolation Hardy derived from 'the limited and severely rationalized Christianity of the late nineteenth century'.[3] He repeatedly disavowed a clear authorial voice in his novels and, no doubt influenced by heavy-handed misinterpretations of his work, was at pains to stress in later prefaces to them that they did not purvey his philosophy of life. In the General

---

[1] Preface to Jude, (1895), p.viii

[2] Writing to the grieving Rider Haggard, whose son had recently died, Hardy conveyed his sympathy but went on to say "...to be candid, I think the death of a child is never really to be regretted, when one reflects on what he has escaped" (CL I p.235).

[3] Orel, p. 118

Preface to the *Wessex Edition* of 1912 he wrote:

> The sentiments in the following pages have been stated truly to be mere impressions of the moment, and not convictions or arguments...

and elsewhere he noted pithily that 'a novel is an impression, not an argument'.[1] In her recent book *Thomas Hardy and His God: A Liturgy of Unbelief* (1991), Deborah Collins has argued cogently that the main spring of Hardy's literary endeavour is the 'polyphonic' (i.e. multivoiced) response to his perception that 'at the centre of man's growing despair and confusion is his inability to fathom the nature of God'.[2] Hardy is analysed in this study as a writer possessed of a number of contradictory voices: one voice is intolerant of Christian dogma, for example, another has a melioristic inclination, whilst a third takes refuge in the ideas of mid-nineteenth century scientific humanism. The poems also provide evidence of varied and even conflicting points of view and belie the charge most often levelled at Hardy that his pages are dominated by pessimism. What was alleged to be 'pessimism', was, he thought, 'only such questionings in the exploration of reality, the first step towards the soul's betterment, and also the body's'; as he put it in verse-

> If way to be Better there be, it exacts a full look at
> the Worse.[3]

However, the poems that deal with religion do become more morose in the final verse-volumes and are inseparably bound up with his sense of the improbability that society could benefit from Christ's example. Writing shortly after the outbreak of the war in August 1914 to his literary executor he noted dejectedly:

> As for myself, the recognition that we are living in a more brutal age than that say. of Elizabeth, or of the chivalry which could cry: 'Gentlemen of the guard, fire first!'...does not inspire one to write hopeful poetry, or even conjectural prose, but simply make one sit still in an apathy, and watch the clock spinning backwards, with a mild wonder if, when it gets back to the Dark Ages, and the sack of Rome, it will ever move forward again to a new Renascence, and a new literature. But people would call this pessimistic so I will stop...[4]

The critic who is disposed to hear the negative voice that encompasses 'the Worst' in Hardy's poetry might well point to <u>Thoughts from Sophocles,</u> and especially <u>A Night of Questionings</u> in which the poet listens in to the exchanges between the

---

[1] Personal Writings, p. 33.

[2] Pp. 1ff., 11ff.

[3] *Apology to Late Lyrics and Earlier* (1922)

[4] CL V, p. 45.

returning souls of the dead and the personified wind on All Soul's Day. All of them, the poor of the parish, high ranking officials, sailors, soldiers and criminals., ask 'What of the world now?' and the wind answers them in variation of '...just as in your time'. Men's nature is unchanged - they 'wander to and fro', 'care little' and 'knave their neighbours' deaths'. And providential religion provides no consolation for human suffering. The Chorus Ironic in The Dynasts mocks at the efficacy of prayer to the Great Heart of the universe in a similarly negative fashion:

> Ha-ha! That's good. Thou'lt pray to It:-
> But where do Its compassions sit?
> Yea, where abides the heart of it?
>
> Is it where sky-fires flame and flit?
> Or solar craters spew and spit
> Or ultra-stellar night-webs knit?
>
> What is its shape? Man's counterfei
> That turns in some far sphere unlit
> The Wheel that drives the Infinite?[1]

Disposed to the positive voice another critic might trace the thread of meliorism which surfaces most spectacularly in the premonition of the Spirit of the Pities in the After Scene of the same epic:

> But - a stirring thrills the air
> Like to sounds of joyance there
>   That the rages
>   Of the ages

Shall be cancelled, and deliverance offered from the darts that were,
Consciousness the Will informing, till it fashion all things fair!
Here is the empathetic heart that reluctantly abjures Christianity and embraces the philosophy of what Hardy himself termed 'evolutionary meliorism'. It must be said, though, that the gross exemplar of man's inhumanity in the First World War 'destroyed all Hardy's belief in the gradual enoblement of man'. In his own words he confessed that he would not have ended The Dynasts as he did 'if he could have foreseen what was going to happens within a few years...'[2] and the poem We are Getting Near the End tilts the balance against the possibility that 'within this universe,/...better whiles may follow worse'. Poems like There Seemed a Strangeness

---

[1] Part Second Act VI, Scene 5.

[2] *The Life, p. 398.*

and <u>Xenophanes the Monist of Colon</u> have a note of hopefulness which is related to the voice of the Spirit of the Pities but this broaches the subject of Hardy's philosophy of the Immanent Will and is not directly concerned with his views on Christianity.

Verses which encapsulate Hardy's lifelong sense of finiteness and change, including the mortality of Christian forms and beliefs deserve mention. In <u>Evening Shadows</u> as the poet watches the shadows of his house lengthen across the garden in the evening sun he reflects that such will go on long after his death - just as, in fact those cast by the ancient British tumulus nearby. As Orel puts it, 'in the evening of his life the shadows lengthen, but when he is dead the shadows will extend no further than now. The shadows of yet living faiths will stretch no farther: all present religions and cultures, including the Christian faith, will fade away': [1]

> And nothing says such shade will spread around
> Even as to-day when men will no more heed
> The Gospel news than when the mound was
> > made.

The poem attacks the notion prevalent among nineteenth century Evangelicals[2] that Christianity among all the world's religions is supreme. Other poems highlight the juxtaposition of pagan and Christian symbols which we saw in <u>Christmas in the Elgin Room</u>. <u>Aquae Sulis</u>, for example, is set in the ruins of the goddess Sul-Minerva's temple at Bath, close by the Abbey Church of St Peter and St Paul. The complaint of the exiled Marbles in the British Museum is echoed in the goddess' protestation against the 'sculptures crude' of Gothic architecture and statuary, the 'despising the joys of man whom I so much loved'. But the Christian god is self-confessedly time-bound too ('You know not', he retorts, 'by what a frail thread we equally hang') and will be looked back on as moribund by future generations ('...I, as you, fail like a song men yesterday sang!'). This recalls the laconic comment of the Spirit of the Years on cathedral ritual:

> A local cult, called Christianity
> Which the wild drama of the wheeling spheres
> Includes, with divers other such, in dim
> Pathetical and brief parentheses;
> Beyond whose reach, uninfluenced, unconcerned,
> The systems of the suns go sweeping on...[3]

---

[1] Orel, p. 120

[2] Hands, p. 89

[3] The Dynasts, Part First, 1, 6; see Hands, p.90 for details in the novels of the Christian usurpation of pagan buildings, a usurpation which in many instances was at best precarious.

Renouncing Christian belief early in his life, Hardy attempted to formulate his own litany of unbelief. Still, if the unequivocal espousal of Darwinism never faltered in his mind, his heart only reluctantly pulled away from the 'bright believing band' of his brethren and the 'mirage mists of their Shining Land'. He never relinquished his passionate concern for the human condition ('What are my books', he once asked, 'but one plea against man's inhumanity to man, to woman and to the lower animals?'), and never failed to sympathize with the disquiet of would-be believers:

We enter church, he wrote, and we have to say, 'We have erred and strayed from Thy ways like lost sheep', when what we want to say is, 'Why are we made to err and stray like lost sheep?' Then we have to sing, 'My soul doth magnify the Lord', when what we want to sing is, 'O that my soul could find some Lord that it could magnify!' Till it can, let us magnify good works, and develop all means of easing mortals' progress through a world not worthy of them. Still, being present, we say the established words full of the historic sentiment only, mentally adding, 'How happy our ancestors were in repeating in all sincerity these articles of faith!'.But we perceive that none of the congregation recognizes that we repeat the words from an antiquarian interest in them, and in a historic sense, and solely to keep a church of some sort afoot - a thing indispensable; so that we are pretending what is not true: that we are believers. This must not be; we must leave. And if we do, we reluctantly go to the door, and creep out as it creaks complainingly behind us.[1]

---

[1] The Life, p. 358

IV *David Jones and Christian Heroism*

– Michael Alexander

David Jones, the somewhat neglected British artist and writer who died in 1974, is the subject of the second half of my lecture. My focus is on his book about the first world war, entitled *In Parenthesis* in allusion to the dates 1914-18, but published only in 1937. I wish to consider this work in the context of Christian heroism, and in the perspective both of English literature of this century and in a longer historical perspective.

There is a literary myth about the poetry of the First World War, of which Wilfrid Owen is both the prophet and the hero. Owen's Preface to his proposed book of poems begins 'This book is not about heroes.... I am not concerned with Poetry. My subject is War, and the pity of War. The Poetry is in the pity'.[1] This last sentence has been very useful to literally millions of our fellowcitizens in an hour of need. Countless examination answers have illustrated Owen's maxim by reference to his own poem, 'Futility'. The pathos of futility is one of the few things left which can make a poem popular. (A parallel example is Edwin's Morgan's poem 'In the Snack Bar'. A few years ago the majority of the Scottish O grade scripts in English answered the question 'Write on a poem which has moved you' by writing about this poem, perhaps provided by their teachers as a nice wee Glasgow poem. It is about a sad character who comes into the snack bar, whom we all feel sorry for but we cannae help.) Wilfred Owen's statement that the Poetry is in the pity has not been universally accepted. The *Oxford Book of Modern Verse* of 1936, for example, excluded Owen with the words, 'Passive suffering is not a theme for poetry.' The author of this Nietzschean dismissal was the editor, W.B.Yeats, the author also of 'An Irish Airman Foresees his Death', for whom poetry lay in heroism. The reflection that poetry lies neither in pity nor in heroism but in words and their arrangement lacks a certain appeal. History tells us that poetry is also to be found in the emotions we may or may not be prepared to supply. The attitude of the editor of the *New Oxford Book of English Verse* of 1973, Philip Larkin, looking back to the first war and to the Cenotaph is markedly patriotic.[2]

If heroism is (to take a short-cut avoiding classical antiquity) a kind of admirable courage often associated with soldiers and held up for emulation, what is Christian

---

[1] *The Collected Poems of Wilfred Owen*, ed. C. Day Lewis, 1963, p. 31.

[2] See for example 'MCMXIV' and 'Naturally the Foundation will Bear Your Expenses' from *The Whitsun Weddings*.

heroism? There may now seem to be some paradox in this combination of words, but Christian heroism is not a contradiction in terms. A hero should enjoy some initial success, but even Achilles ends the <u>Iliad</u> by conceding his own mortality and failure; and in the <u>Odyssey</u> he says to Odysseus in Hades that it is better to be the slave of a slave in the land of the living than the greatest in the world of the dead. The greatest of heroes must die, indeed their deaths are what make them representatively human, and it is often the nature of their deaths, and the cause in which they die which makes them heroic. But the earthly career of the person whom Christians follow ended in abject worldly failure and a degrading form of death by public torture. Before the emperor Constantine early Christianity boasted heroes whom we rather think of as martyrs; but mediaeval Christendom reconciled these ideals. Here is the beginning of an Anglo-Saxon poem of some local interest in St. Andrews, in the translation of C W Kennedy.[1]

> Lo! We have heard of twelve mighty heroes
> Honoured under heaven in days of old,
> Thanes of God. Their glory failed not
> In the clash of banners, the brunt of war,
> After they were scattered and spread abroad
> As their lots were cast by the Lord of heaven.
> Famous those heroes, foremost on earth,
> Brave-hearted leaders and bold in strife
> When hand and buckler defended the helm
> On the plain of war; on the field of fate.
>
> One was Matthew....

Andreas presents the twelve apostles as the <u>comitatus</u> of a Germanic lord. To modern eyes they may look more like a commando unit.

A form of Christian heroism more acceptable today is to be found in the very early Anglo-Saxon poem *The Dream of the Rood*, where the Redeemer himself is presented as a <u>geong haeleth</u>, a young hero, eager to meet death. The core text of the poem is carried on the Ruthwell Cross, dated *c.* 700 A.D.

---

[1] C.W.Kennedy, *Early English Christian Poetry*, London, 1952, p.122.

Lines 39-41 of *The Dream of the Rood.* Inscription in water-colours, 1952, reproduced as the final illustration in *The Anathemata* (1954). Literally :

'The young hero who was God Almighty ungirded himself, strong and determined; he mounted on the high gallows, brave in the sight of many, when he wished to redeem mankind'. See *David Jones*, ed. Paul Hills, Tate Gallery, London, 1981, p. 131. The best edition of *The Dream of the Rood* is that of Michael Swanson, 1970, 1987.

In the fourteenth century poem, *Piers Plowman*, Christ going to his crucifixion is presented as a knight entering the lists in the armour of human nature.

> 'This Jesus of his gentrice wole juste in Piers armes,
> In his helme and in his haberjoun, <u>humana</u> <u>natura</u>.'

(This Jesus in his nobility wishes to joust in the arms of Piers, in his helmet and his coat of mail — human nature.)[1] But Constantine's adoption of the cross as the standard of earthly armies ended with the last crusade; or so it seemed to Renaissance humanists and Reformers contemplating Julius II, and Protestant historians writing about the Conquistadores. Evelyn Waugh, General Aoun, and some Ukrainians and Croatians might not agree. For Milton, who inherited the Renaissance definition of epic as a poem exemplifying heroism, true heroism consisted in 'patience and heroic martyrdom', more passive than active.[2] During Cromwell's <u>aristeia</u> this had not always been Milton's opinion, but during the 1650s the cause of paradise on earth had been gradually lost. But only since the first world war, the war called great, has a significant proportion of thoughtful Christians in established churches become, like many other thoughtful persons, pacifist or pro-pacifist and anti-war. This was partly a result of that war.

The British soldiers of the trench war have been seen in retrospect as lions led by donkeys. One of my grandfathers died in the trenches, the other was gassed, which limited his life after the war. The awfulness of that war led to a horror of war which can be held to blame for some of the political misjudgements of the thirties. It is not too much of a parody to present the popularized literary history of that war as a boxing match. In the blue corner the pre-match favourite, Brooke's 'The Soldier' (containing the patriotic words 'there's some corner of a foreign field /That is forever England'). In the red corner the protest poetry of Owen, Sassoon and Rosenberg. The result, in the opinion of most subsequent literary judges, though not of everyone in the crowd either then or now, has been a knock-out. Hindsight seemed to show Brooke's idealism as mistaken, and the outraged protest of Owen and Sassoon at the trauma of the trenches has led, historically, to an English cult of their work. It is becoming clear that the literary, as distinct from the moral, merit of that work has been overrated: the canon of this war poetry is tiny and its merit is modest in comparison with its subsequent reputation and effect. Whatever the shortcomings of their poetry, this strange trio of Owen, Sassoon and Rosenberg

---

[1] Piers Plowman B-Version, Passus 18, 23-4. The Middle Ages, Vol. 1 of the *Macmillan Anthologies of English Literature*, ed. Alexander, M. and Riddy, F., London, 1989, p. 209.

[2] *Paradise Lost*, IX, 32.

gave courageous and necessary expression to the trauma caused by mechanized slaughter after a long age of liberal peace. Owen hopes in his Preface that the spirit of his poetry would 'survive Prussia'. He and Sassoon returned to the front and to another form of heroism.

It is a curiosity of the way literary history has been written that three contemporary groups of writers, the modernists T S Eliot and Ezra Pound, the war-poets Owen and Sassoon, and the Bloomsbury Woolfs and Forster have traditionally been treated separately. This draws attention away from the truth that the war poets were scarcely modern in style. The modernists Pound, Eliot and Joyce were aliens and noncombatants whose art had little to say about the war at the time. Pound was only agreeing with many others when he noted in *Hugh Selwyn Mauberley* that the war was such that it was neither sweet nor proper to die for the fatherland. Eliot's first volume *Prufrock and Other Observations* is dedicated to a friend who died at the Dardanelles, and *The Waste Land* could be regarded as an oblique elegy to the human and spiritual losses of the war; but it makes specific reference only to the destruction of the Austro-Hungarian empire and its consequences. It is clear in retrospect that Pound's *Cantos* are a lifetime's effort to account for how the cultural, social and economic history of the West led to the First World War. In this he was no more successful than other ethical economists in the thirties. The tertium quid, Bloomsbury, may not have been as unpatriotic as is often claimed, but the priority they famously accorded to personal relationships might be interpreted as an avoidance of the war.

Nearly all subsequent literature directly about the 1914-18 war was unheroic or antiheroic and non-Christian. David Jones's *In Parenthesis* is therefore atypical in three ways among war books. It is heroic, it is Christian, and it is also modernist, both in its fragmented style and in its ambitious historical perspective. It appeared in 1937 to some applause ('a work of genius' — T S Eliot. Evelyn Waugh wrote that it had 'a painter's realism which lifts' Jones's work 'above any of Mr Eliot's followers and, in many places, above Mr Eliot himself. Moreover Jones has a painter's communicativeness.' A later work of Jones's, *The Anathemata* (1954), was regarded by W.H.Auden as the finest long poem of the century, partly perhaps because it offers a syncretic Christian synthesis of Western history.) But *In Parenthesis* has not found favour with such recent critics as Paul Fussell or Jon Silkin. What they cannot accept or understand is the analogy Jones draws with earlier wars, some of them heroic and chivalric; for this refuses the traumatic claim of the literature which protested that this particular war was absolutely unprecedented, uniquely senseless and an experience without the possibility of redeeming significance. But for a Welshman like David Jones, who as a little boy had spat on the tomb of Edward I in Westminster Abbey, and for a Christian, the war was not unprecedented. In a recent anthology of the prose of the first world war Jon Silkin quotes from Jones's introduction to *In Parenthesis*: 'The wholesale slaughter of the later years... knocked the bottom out of the intimate, continuing domestic life of small contingents of men, within whose structure Roland could find, and, for a reasonable while, enjoy, his Oliver.' This last sentence reduces Silkin to incoherence.[1] The *Chanson de Roland*, with the heroic friendship of Roland and Oliver, is an impermissible analogy to the first war because it is a prototype of crusade-literature, with a sacred Christian cause, a fighting bishop, devilish muslims, and Christian heroes. It is surely a matter of record, however, that Owen for a reasonable while enjoyed his Sassoon; war did not end friendship. I also know of at least one person who took the *Chanson* with him to the Spanish Civil War and who died fighting for the republican side. For him Franco and his African troops may have corresponded to the mohammedans of the old poem. Jones in his introduction also mentions Shakespeare's *Henry V*, a play which in the next war Winston Churchill and Laurence Olivier were to put to patriotic use. Such a usage seems to have put Shakespeare himself out of court for some readers, especially for those who were especially opposed to Nazism. In *Henry IV* Shakespeare has Glendower say: 'I can call spirits from the vasty deep.' The English Hotspur replies: 'And so can I and so can any man, but will they come when you do call for them?' (III.i.53-5). There are modern readers who would prefer that spirits (if there are any) should on no account be called for.   I am far more concerned with the modern deafness towards David Jones. This is not an age in which outstanding British poets have been too thick on the ground.

Jones wrote *In Parenthesis* in a time when he could not paint; he was recovering from a nervous breakdown. Literary modernism, or the modern movement as I prefer to call it, deals with the breakdown of modern European culture marked though not caused by the war, and attempts to establish ambitious literary syntheses of universal import. I am distrustful of Hegelian efforts to explain cultural history by a dialectic of isms. By the modern movement in literature I merely mean *The Waste Land* and *Ulysses* and perhaps *Women in Love*, all published in 1922, and the *Cantos* of Ezra Pound. The work of Joyce, Eliot and Pound has all been said to use a comparative mythical method, described by Eliot in his review of *Ulysses*.[2] *The Waste Land* achieves universality at some cost to actuality; Kingsley Amis

---

[1] Quoted and attacked in *The Penguin Book of First World War Prose*, ed. Jon Glover and Jon Silkin, London, 1988, p. 8-9. See also Paul Fussell, *The Great War and Modern Memory*, London, 1975.

[2] T.S.Eliot, *"Ulysses, Order and Myth"*, Dial, lxx.5 (Nov. 1923), 483. See Ronald Bush, *T.S.Eliot*, New York and London, 1988, p. 71-2.

complained that there are not enough advertisements in Eliot's version of the London Underground. This crack must be provoked by Eliot's mock-solemn notes, such as this one, to line 218: 'Just as the one-eyed merchant, seller of currants, melts into the Phoenician sailor, but the latter is not wholly distinct from Ferdinand, Prince of Naples, so all the women are one woman.' 'That is at least one definite "false note"', as Eliot himself wrote in *Portrait of a Lady*. Nor can I be the only reader of the poem who finds that the myth of the Fisher King works only intermittently.

How does this 'mythic method' work in Jones? *In Parenthesis* benefits from our knowledge of the Great War, part of the common *data* of the twentieth century. It also tells a story, much more of a story than do the *Cantos* or *The Waste Land*, and more simply than does Joyce in *Ulysses*. As a narrative, it succeeds far better than theirs do, and it succeeds in becoming the inclusive narrative archetype of the infantryman's experience of going up to the Front.

One factor in Jones's success in generalizing the experience he renders in *In Parenthesis* is that it is common experience, experienced by him as a common soldier. Another is that he meditated upon it for ten years or more before writing it out. There is no loss of immediacy in the rendering of action or of language, and the descriptions have all the detail as well as the orderly disposition of a painting. But in the general analogies—whether historical, literary, mythical or religious— which are constantly offered there is, evidently, an ever deepening dimension without, for the most part, any loss of actuality, though some of the Celtic boasting and fantasy is consciously put into the form of a dream.

An example from the Night Watch passage, from *In Parenthesis* part 3:
>   And the rain slacks at the wind veer
>   and she half breaks her cloud cover.
> He puts up a sufficient light dead over the Neb; and in its moments
> hanging, star-still, shedding a singular filament of peace, for these fantastic
> undulations.
> He angled rigid; head and shoulders free; his body's inclination at the
> extreme thrust of the sap head; outward toward them, like the calm breasts
> of her, silent above the cutwater, foremost toward them
> and outmost of us, and
> brother-keeper, and ward-watcher;
> his mess-mates sleeping like long-barrow sleepers, their dark arms at reach.

The night sentry is Jones's and our representative, John Ball, a name as English as David Jones's was Welsh, which must have been chosen in reminiscence of the priest who was one of the leaders of the Peasants' Revolt in 1381. Our protagonist is 'outward toward them'. 'They' are the German enemy, who are also the 'He' who 'puts up a sufficient light' over John Ball. 'She' is the moon, who, like everything else in No Man's Land, has been militarized, and 'half breaks her cloud cover'. Her light makes the swell of the chalky downs and the lines of the trenches seem like the sea's 'fantastic undulations', and the figure guarding the English saphead turns into a female figurehead breasting the moonstruck waves. This play with pronouns domesticates and familiarises Jones's imaginative projections, so that the enemy, the moon, and the landscape all become personal and natural. No Man's Land becomes Everyman's Land. There is a keen sense of personal space, location and identity but at the same time a radiation of universal sympathies appropriated into familial relations. The inclusive use of personal pronouns – constant in *In Parenthesis* – may owe something to T. S. Eliot's example in *The Waste Land*, though here put to a less disturbing effect. The moonlight makes the sleeping mess-mates seem to Ball like the fairy heroes who in legend sleep under the historical tumuli of Britain. The 'ward-watcher' is also (what Cain was not to Abel) his brother's keeper. And the German light hangs like the star over Bethlehem, singularly promising peace to men (it is the eve of that Christmas when the front lines exchanged presents). This is a midwinter night's dream, full of myth and metamorphosis.

In a passage which follows soon after, the moon's powers increase:

> You can hear the silence of it:
> you can hear the rat of no-man's-land
>   rut-out intricacies,
> weasel-out his patient workings,
> scrut, scrut, scrut,
> harrow-out earthly, trowel his cunning paw;
> redeem the time of our uncharity, to sap his own amphibious paradise.
>   You can hear his carrying-parties rustle our corruptions through the night-
> weeds—contest the choicest morsels in his tiny conduits, bead-eyed feast on us;
> by a rule of his nature, at night-feast on the broken of us.
>   Those broad-pinioned;
> blue-burnished, or brinded-back;
> whose proud eyes watched
>   the broken emblems
> droop and drag dust,

suffer with us this metamorphosis.

These too have shed their fine feathers; these too have slimed their dark-bright coats; these too have condescended to dig in.

The white-tailed eagle at the battle ebb,

                          where the sea wars against the river

the speckled kite of Maldon

and the crow

have naturally selectcd to be un-winged;

 to go on the belly, to

sap   sap   sap

with festered spines, arched under the moon; furrit with whiskered snouts the secret parts of us.

When it's all quiet you can hear them:

scrut scrut scrut

When it's as quiet as this is.

    It's so very still.

    Your body fits thc crevice of thc bay in the most

comfortable fashion imaginable.

    It's cushy enough.

    The relief elbows him on the fire-step: All quiet china?—

bugger all to report?— kipping mate?— christ, mate — you'll 'ave 'em all over.

Here the 'You' includes everyone addressed in the audience: the innocent Jones treats the reader as an intimate. The rat too is considered with sympathy, as a fellow creature caught up in the war, who feasts on us 'by a rule of his nature'. By a similar mental habit of inclusiveness, demonstrative adjectives are used like the pronouns, with the simplicity of an oral narrative: 'Those broad-pinioned' birds of prey of the battlefields of old have become 'These' rodents of no-man's-land. *The Battle of Maldon,* an Anglo-Saxon poem commemorating the battle fought against the Vikings at Maldon in Essex in A. D. 991, begins with the East Saxon commander sending away the horses and bidding his men advance. A young warrior then lets his hawk fly to the wood from his wrist, betokening the exchanging of the pursuits of peace for the weapons of war. Later in the poem the ravens and the eagle circle above the battlefield as the ebb tide goes out and the armies engage. Jones particularises: the young warrior's 'beloved hawk' becomes a 'speckled kite'; he incorporates the white-tailed eagle from *The Battle of Brunanburh.* But he also makes a new general myth: the noble air-borne beasts of heroic battle where men stood up to fight by day have become the underground night-fighters of the trogloditic trench-war. The process of natural selection is represented as an anti-heroic degeneration not an improving evolution: like modern men, the birds have 'condescended to digin'. This feeling that modern industrial life expressed in the War represents a Fall is common to many of the Modernists: Eliot, and Pound (and Lawrence). But Jones humorously regards the rats as fellow creatures who, in order to live, have to sap their own conduits, just like men. For him the continuities with the suffering warriors of the past and with the sufferings of the creation, are, despite the metamorphoses, more essential than the discontinuities.

The final passage I have chosen to illustrate this theme is from Part 7 of *In Parenthesis*.

> The returning sun climbed over the hill, to lessen the shadows of small
> and great things; and registered the minutes to zero hour. Their saucer
> hats made dial for his passage: long thin line of them, virid domes of
> them,
> cut elliptical with light
> as cupola on Byzantine wall,
> stout turrets to take the shock
> and helmets of salvation.
> Long side by side lie like friends lie
> on daisy-down on warm days
> cuddled close down kindly close with the mole
> in down and silky rodent,
> and if you look more intimately all manner of small creatures,
> created-dear things creep about quite comfortably
> yet who travail until now
> beneath your tin-hat shade.
>   He bawls at ear-hole:
> Two minutes to go.
>   Minutes to excuse me to make excuse.
> Responde mihi?
>   for surely I must needs try them
> so many, much undone
> and lose on roundabouts as well and vari-coloured polygram
> to love and know
>   and we have a little sister
> whose breasts will be as towers
> and the gilly-flowers will blow next month
> below the pound
> with Fred Karno billed for *The Holloway*.

The gentle slopes are green to remind you
of South English places, only far wider and flatter spread and
grooved and harrowed criss-cross whitely and the disturbed
subsoil heaped up albescent.

Across upon this undulated board of verdure chequered bright
when you look to left and right
small, drab, bundled pawns severally make effort
moved in tenuous line
and if you looked behind—the next wave came slowly, as suc-
cessive surfs creep in to dissipate on flat shore;
and to your front, stretched long laterally,
and receded deeply,
the dark wood.

And now the gradient runs more flatly toward the separate
scarred saplings, where they make fringe for the interior
thicket
and you take notice.
       There between the thinning uprights
at the margin
straggle tangled oak and flayed sheeny beech-bole, and fragile
birch whose silver queenery is draggled and ungraced
and June shoots lopt
and fresh stalks bled
       runs the Jerry trench.
And cork-screw stapled trip-wire
to snare among the briars
and iron warp with bramble weft
with meadow-sweet and lady-smock
for a fair camouflage.

Mr. Jenkins half inclined his head to them – he walked just barely in
advance of his platoon and immediately to the left of Private Ball.

  He makes the conventional sign
and there is the deeply inward effort of spent men who would
make response for him,

and take it at the double.
He sinks on one knee
and now on the other,
his upper body tilts in rigid inclination
this way and back;
weighted lanyard runs out to full tether,
        swings like a pendulum
        and the clock run down.
Lurched over, jerked iron saucer over tilted brow
clampt unkindly over lip and chin
nor no ventaille to this darkening
        the masked face lifts to grope the air
and so disconsolate;
enfeebled fingering at a paltry strap —
buckle holds,
holds him blind against the morning.
    Then stretch still where weeds pattern the chalk predella –
where it rises to his wire – and Sergeant T. Quilter takes over.

The death of Lt. Jenkins is heroic as well as pathetic, it is not pointless, it is offered a Christian perspective. <u>Responde mihi</u> are the imagined words of Christ from the Cross which conclude each of the series of <u>Improperia</u> or Reproaches in the Good Friday liturgy of the Catholic Church . The 'chalk predella' onto which Mr Jenkins 'sinks on one knee' is a kneeler . Which means, in the retrospect of the reader, that the 'conventional sign' the lieutenant makes is not only the sign to advance but also the sign of the cross. Further, the words 'nor no ventaille to this darkening', alluding to the visor of a mediaeval helmet, express an incorporation of the life of the <u>miles Christi</u> into the knightly code, forever associated in English literature with the work of Sir Thomas Malory's *Morte Arthure*. The Victorian reappropriation of Arthurian chivalry to the code of the English Christian gentleman, by Tennyson and others, was one of the incidental casualties of the Somme. But, like Arthur, the gentleman will not lie quiet.

On the whole, the kind of heroic dimension offered by Jones is not individual but collective and retrospective, applying to the most surprising people. Ball is the protagonist, not the hero, a Tommy Atkins follower and a narrative centre of consciousness, not a leader, and certainly not the kind of 'hero' of popular romantic literature with whom we are to sympathise and whom we are to admire almost uncritically. He's rather a wimp; and though he fights well, he eventually runs or crawls away. Ball is wounded in the attack on Mametz Wood, shot in the leg, and crawls away, most unheroically leaving his rifle, the 'last personal arm'. But there is a pastoral sequel in the final pages in which the Queen of the Woods, a figure with analogies to Diana, to the Blessed Virgin Mary and to Shakespeare's Perdita, awards flowers to the 'secret princes', reconciling the fallen in the 'undercrypt' of the wood. There are, as I say, some surprising awards: 'That swine Lilywhite has daisies to his chain — you'd hardly credit it.' The fallen Welsh are treated as scapebeasts for the fratricidal blindness of 'the square-heads', the English and the Germans. The secret princes are thus enrolled not only in a Christian litany of remembrance but also into a new version of the chivalric legend of British history. It is important to make it clear that this litany of remembrance and this chivalric legend do not deny the present misery, the suffering or the unintelligible waste. Though the point may not have been evident to those who fell, their sacrifice is not presented as pointless. The kind of heroism implied is not glorious nor particularly valorous, more a question of putting up with it. In this quality of endurance it resembles martyrdom as much as heroism. The cause is obscure, there is a sense of duty rather than of the need to resist German militarism or to 'survive Prussia'. And the kind of Christianity implied is of the most inclusive sort. Jones's notion of the Catholic Church was that it included, as he would say, many chaps who did not know they were in it.

The experience of the extraordinary life of the ordinary soldier came to have a sustaining significance for David Jones, especially in the light of the religious position he adopted after the war, in which the necessity for accepting suffering, cheerfully if possible, was a tenet. The significance and order Jones eventually made out, with a painful and continuing difficulty, was the product of years of patiently living with his experiences. Perhaps this lecture has not been concerned so much with heroism and Christianity as with the admissibility in our century of finding redeeming significance in suffering, and the admissibility of continuing to find any sacramental symbolic dimension or any metaphysical analogy for the godforsaken life and death of the trenches. The broken texture of *In Parenthesis*, its relapse into prose, may be related to the intense strain of finding any formal analogy in human and sacred history to the dire actuality of a subject matter which did not easily yield meaning, still less the moral grandeur of heroism. The soldiers of the First World War were not, of course, the first soldiers or men to feel themselves godforsaken. On the cross Jesus himself quoted the opening of Psalm 22, traditionally attributed to King David, who lived a thousand years earlier: 'My God, my God, why hast thou forsaken me?' Such continuities held David Jones, who quoted a line from the Dies irae which allowed him to associate his Christian name with King David and with the Sybil of Virgil's Messianic Eclogue: TESTE DAVID CUM SIBYLLA.

V   Doubt and Belief in
Dostoevsky's Major Novels

– R. F. Christian

Many Russian writers and thinkers of this century, both in Russia and abroad, have prided themselves - rightly in my opinion - on the richness of their 19th century literary legacy, and especially the 19th century Russian novel. They have emphasised - with perhaps a touch of smugness - their literature's greater 'humaneness' and greater preoccupation with serious religious and political problems than was the case with other European prose fiction of the time. Gogol, who wrote Russia's greatest comic and satirical novel *Dead Souls*, was obsessed with the fear of death and hell, and came to believe that he had a divine mission to divert his literary talents to the cause of the moral regeneration of his sinful country. Consequently, in an attempt to repair the damage he thought *Dead Souls* had caused through the triumph of its hero, the arch-rogue Chichikov, he began to write a second part designed to bring about his moral regeneration. Soon afterwards Gogol made a pilgrimage to the Holy Land, but when he failed to experience the religious inspiration he had sought, he burned some of his manuscripts including much of the sequel to *Dead Souls,* and died in a state of morbid melancholy. Gogol's death coincided exactly with the literary debut of Tolstoy, whose novels, and especially his later stories and articles, reflected his troubled search for a meaning to life which his own death would not negate. Maxim Gorky once said that Tolstoy's uneasy relations with God reminded him of the relations of 'two bears in one den'[1]. In *War and Peace* Pierre is beset with doubts and torments, a 'seeker' endlessly searching for a way of life which would have some purpose beyond the mere satisfaction of his instincts and desires. In *Anna Karenina* Levin takes Pierre's quest a stage further and manages to reason himself into a sort of spiritual equilibrium where reason is not all important, and where the words of a simple peasant about the need to live for God and one's soul have at least a temporary impact. The last part of *Anna Karenina* leads logically into Tolstoy's profession of faith *A Confession*, which in turn leads on to his *Criticism of Dogmatic Theology,* his *Translation and Harmony of the Gospels* (for which he diligently studied Greek and Hebrew), and his later religious writings.

---

[1] *Reminiscences of Leo Nikolaevich Tolstoy,* 1919, reprinted in Katherine Mansfield, S.S.Koteliansky and Leonard Woolf (translated) *Reminiscences of Tolstoy, Chekhov and Andreev,*1934, XVII

But nobody in Russia went as far as Dostoevsky in integrating literature and religion in major works of fiction - Dostoevsky, 'a child of the age', as he called himself, 'a child of unbelief and doubt', with a terrible 'craving to believe'[1]; a man, as he later said, tormented consciously or unconsciously all his life by the problem of the existence of God.

E.H. Carr, the historian and biographer of Dostoevsky, once wrote in a review:- 'Dostoevsky has always presented a problem to his biographers. He died in 1881 in an odour of religious and political sanctity, which exhaled more than a whiff of national chauvinism and anti-semitism; and the orthodoxy of his last years and writings redeemed the radical sins of his youth, expiated by nearly ten years in Siberia[2].'

The story of Dostoevsky's life is a fascinating one, but today when I am concerned mainly with his fiction, I can only refer fairly briefly to a few stages in his apparent progression from sinner to saint. Dostoevsky's early home environment was not a happy one. His father seems to have been a cruel, evil-tempered, debauched dipsomaniac, who is believed to have been murdered by his serfs - although the evidence is not conclusive. Certainly Dostoevsky himself believed the story, and there is no doubt that he was abnormally interested in a son's attitude towards his father and the crime of parricide. While the young Dostoevsky was obviously not responsible for his father's death, he may have wished for it (as Ivan Karamazov did in Dostoevsky's last novel). He may perhaps have felt that <u>he</u> had been made to suffer for his father's sins. He may have thought that his own bad temper, moodiness, suspiciousness, even viciousness, and early proneness to debauchery were really his father's fault - the sins of the fathers being visited upon the children. And it would not be naive to see a connection between Dostoevsky's unhappy home life and his father's murder on the one hand, and on the other hand, the exploration of the father/son relationship and the theme of parricide in his greatest novel *The Brothers Karamazov*.

If Dostoevsky's life started unpromisingly, his path to maturity was quite exceptionally difficult. In the late 1840s he began to get involved with dissident political circles in Petersburg, whether a relatively innocent one which discussed among other things the merits of French utopian socialism, or a more active revolutionary group which met regularly to consider ways of spreading general

---

[1] Letter to N.D.Fonvizina, February, 1854, in *Dostoevsky's Letters*, translated and edited David Lowe and Ronald Meyer, Vol. 1, 1988, pp. 193ff.

[2] *Times Literary Supplement*, 30 September, 1977

dissatisfaction, as he said, with the existing order in Russia, and at which he admitted to having been guilty of the intention (but no more) to act against the government. The consequences of this youthful academic radicalism were dire in the extreme. He was sentenced to death in 1849, and only reprieved at the very last moment when virtually face to face with the firing squad. He spent the next four years in penal servitude in Siberia, and five more on compulsory army service there. When he returned to European Russia in 1859 and resumed his journalistic activities, the two literary periodicals with which he was associated either failed or were closed down by the authorities. His favourite brother died. The nervous seizures from which he had suffered for many years proved to be epilepsy, and matters were not improved when he had a severe epileptic fit immediately after his marriage to his first wife, who subsequently became a hysterical neurotic. The marriage officially lasted for seven years, but long before her death Dostoevsky had left her for a stormy affair with a certain Apollinaria Suslova - a capricious, vindictive, 'diabolical' woman who left her mark on Polina in Dostoevsky's story *The Gambler*, the type of woman frequently encountered in his later novels, capable of simultaneous love and hatred and perversely alternating between kindness and cruelty. He indulged in gambling orgies, became bankrupt and eventually left Russia in 1867, possibly to escape imprisonment for debt, with his second wife whom he had married after a number of brief liaisons with other women, and who remained his faithful and devoted companion for the rest of his life.

Having been attracted as a young man to the belief that men could plan their own happiness without God, Dostoevsky swung round politically to what would nowadays be called a reactionary, right-wing position, from which he mocked the radicals and satirised the revolutionaries (in *The Devils*), demolished the concept of planned happiness in *the Brothers Karamazov* and came to identify socialism with atheism and anti-Christ. Towards the end of his life, this ex-political convict was hobnobbing with royalty. The Tsar himself let it be known that he wanted Dostoevsky to meet his younger sons and exercise a beneficial influence on them by his talks. In addition, he was on very friendly terms with Pobedonostsev, the reactionary Procurator of the Holy Synod, with whom he exchanged some important letters about the religious and political ideas in *The Brothers Karamazov*.

One of Dostoevsky's fundamental ideas which he elaborated in both his journalism and fiction was his deep-rooted belief in the 'Russian people' ('*narod*' in Russian, meaning the broad masses of the peasantry, uncontaminated by Catholicism, the Reformation or the crude materialism of Western European civilisation) and in the 'truth' which they allegedly express - *narodnaya pravda*. His faith in the Russian *narod* (despite his frequent strictures about their drunkenness and barbarity) was closely linked with his belief in their profoundly religious nature - the very opposite view to that of his older contemporary, the enormously influential literary critic and pioneer of Russian socialism, Vissarion Belinsky, who believed the Russians to be the most atheistic of all peoples! Towards the end of his life Dostoevsky became increasingly chauvinistic, xenophobic and anti-semitic. He had always been rather contemptuous of foreigners and most of what he saw outside Russia, and the frequent references in his letters to revolting Yids, stupid Germans, nauseating Frenchmen, banal and uncivilised Swiss, trashy little Poles and ugly English mugs, are unlikely to make him popular with the European Commissioners. D.H. Lawrence called him 'a rotten little stinker'[1] - though perhaps he was not the best person to say so! He believed that the Russian people had an innate capacity to respond to all that was best in Europe without ceasing to be truly Russian; that they had a divine mission to unite the whole of the Orthodox Slavonic world under Russia's wing for the ultimate benefit of mankind; and that this mission was to be the answer to all Europe's -isms, against which he inveighed unsparingly in many of his writings. He was an implacable enemy of Catholicism, which he virtually equated with socialism and totalitarianism, and one of his recent biographers was to write that Dostoevsky's mind later became 'a confused battleground on which various negative stimuli such as Atheists, Catholics, Socialists, Communists, Jesuits, Jews and stockbrokers were locked in conflict with other, positive stimuli such as the Orthodox, the Russian, the Slav and the *narod'*[2].

For the Soviets, at least until recently, Dostoevsky's reactionary political views and his so-called religious obscurantism made him a difficult author to accommodate - particularly since Lenin had had nothing to say on his behalf - and various forms of censorship were practised to prevent his works from corrupting the youth. The Soviet literary establishment feared that his novels might generate an unhealthy interest in religion - while my old headmaster, from the opposite corner as it were - warned us against reading *The Brothers Karamazov* as a book likely to undermine one's faith!

A word now about Dostoevsky's religious background. He knew his Bible extremely well - indeed there were times during his years in prison when the authorities allowed him to read nothing but the Bible - and his copy of the New Testament, heavily marked and underlined, can still be seen in the Lenin Library. From the Old Testament, the Book of Job affected him profoundly. His immensely wide reading included the writings of the Church Fathers, ecclesiastical history and

---

[1] Letter to S.S.Koteliansky, 15 December, 1916

[2] Ronald Hingley, *The Undiscovered Dostoyevsky*, 1962, p. 180

the lives of the saints. After a period of indifference, his early religious faith was reawakened in Siberia from where he wrote in a famous letter that the greater the arguments against his craving to believe the stronger that craving became, and that if anyone should prove to him 'that Christ was outside the truth and if it *really* was the case that the truth was outside Christ, then I'd rather remain with Christ than with the truth'[1]. Like Tolstoy - whom Lenin called 'a jaded, hysterical sniveller, obsessed with Christ'[2] - Dostoevsky was tormented by religion. But their differences were very great. Tolstoy's religious conversion, if that is what it was, was largely motivated by pride - he sought in religion an antidote to his excessive egotism and looked to it for a set of rules, a guide to conduct, a way to improve himself morally and become a better man. For Dostoevsky on the other hand, the motive force was rather pity - pity for human suffering. Dostoevsky balked rationally at Christianity as much as Tolstoy did. But through his own suffering and his observation of the suffering of others he groped painfully towards a spiritual faith quite different from Tolstoy's *ethical* concern with moral codes and rules of behaviour.

After this long introduction, I want to turn now to the more important works of fiction which reflect Dostoevsky's religious doubts, but also his determination to believe.

It is commonly accepted that *Notes from Underground* is the prologue to the five major novels which Dostoevsky wrote between 1866 and 1880, starting with *Crime and Punishment* and culminating in *The Brothers Karamazov* - a dividing line between his early pre-Siberian stories of the 1840s in which the characters are essentially passive, and the great post-Siberian novels with their heroes in revolt against God, the nature of the universe or simply the laws and conventions of society. It contains the seeds of so much that bears fruit in the next 15 years: the problem of free will and authority, the positive and negative sides of the unlimited exercise of the will, the fallacies of the concept of planned happiness, the salutary value of suffering - but not as yet, the ultimate need for belief in God.

Notes from Underground is a work of quite exceptional importance in the history of modern European literature. To quote Joseph Frank, Dostoevsky's most comprehensive biographer:- 'Few works in modern literature are more widely read or more often cited than Dostoevsky's *Notes*. The designation "underground man", has entered into the vocabulary of the modern educated consciousness, and this

---

[1] Letter to Fonvizina (note 1, p. 72)

[2] "Leo Tolstoy as the Mirror of the Russian Revolution", 1908, reprinted in Leo Tolstoy, *Penguin Critical Anthologies*, edited Henry Gifford, 1971, p. 135

character has now begun - like Hamlet, Don Quixote, Don Juan and Faust - to take on the symbolic stature of one of the great archetypal literary creations. Every important cultural development of the last half-century - Nietzscheanism, Freudianism, Expressionism, Surrealism, Crisis Theology, Existentialism - has claimed the "underground man" as its own'...[1]

The *Notes* fall into two halves: Part I which is a first person soliloquy by a lonely, neurotic and hypersensitive introvert - the so-called underground man - in which he expounds his philosophy of life; and Part 2 - a narrative in which the metaphysics of the first part give way to morbid psychology, as the underground man recounts some of the more disreputable actions which his theories have led him to commit.

The hero of the *Notes*, or anti-hero, as Dostoevsky calls him, is spiteful, selfish, masochistic, mentally and morally sick. The gist of his philosophy is that there are two categories of people: normal people, and those, like himself, of heightened awareness. Men of heightened awareness are men of inaction. The fruit of thinking too much is inertia. The underground man, having *reasoned* himself into a state of inertia, then attacks *reason* - but the reason he attacks is rationalism, especially its 19th century manifestations - positivism, utilitarianism, enlightened self-interest, utopian socialism. He attacks the type of scientific determinism symbolised for him by the laws of arithmetic, inescapable truisms such as 2x2=4, or the inexorable laws of nature. He attacks the whole idea of the brave new world, planned happiness, the building of the crystal palace; and above all he attacks the utilitarian belief that reasonable people will always act in accordance with their own interests - that once they know what is good for them they will always do it. He attacks his two targets of 'reason' and 'interest' (i.e. one's own interest) because they allegedly curb freedom - freedom to object to 2x2=4; freedom to demolish the man-made crystal palace; freedom to hurt yourself if you want to; freedom to do irrational things just for the sake of it. 'Man not only may', he says at one point, 'but sometimes positively must act against his own interests'.

Loathsome and neurotic as he is, the underground man states his case against determinism in the name of freedom of the will. But even *he* has to acknowledge at the end that freedom has been too heavy a burden for men to bear; and in a significant and revealing sentence at the very end of the book he feels obliged to say: 'give us more independence, loosen our hands, widen the sphere of our activity, weaken the guardianship, and I assure you we'll at once beg to be taken back into guardianship' - a sentence which prepares the ground for the famous Grand Inquisitor Legend in *The Brothers Karamazov,* which I shall come to shortly. It seems that Dostoevsky wanted to go further than the underground man in

---

[1] Joseph Frank, *Dostoevsky. The Stir of Liberation* (1860 - 1865), 1986, p. 310

attacking rationalism and determinism, and to make the point that the 19th century planners had left God out of the reckoning. Ironically enough, he told his brother that the censors had left in the passages where he mocked and blasphemed and cut out the part where he deduced the need for a belief in Christ. This part has not survived; but it is reasonable to assume that it was the consequences of the unfettered exercise of the will which drove Dostoevsky to acknowledge the need not for a *temporal* but for a *spiritual* authority, and ultimately the Russian Orthodox Christian God. What particularly intrigued Dostoevsky was the fate of people who exercise their will to the limits - the Napoleons, the supermen - and more especially the consequences of the belief that if there is no will beyond my own -if there is no God - then I am my own God and am entitled to exercise my own will without restraint.

The problems raised in the *Notes* by the obnoxious, unbalanced, neurotic anti-hero, who nevertheless voices some fundamental beliefs of Dostoevsky, will figure prominently in the major novels, beginning with *Crime and Punishment.* The outstanding Russian literary critic of this century, Prince Mirsky, who after some years in London as an émigré, rashly went back to the USSR and perished in the camps, suggested at least four ways of reading these novels.[1] One was the way of Dostoevsky's own contemporaries - to relate them to the current issues of Russian life between 1865 and 1880 - the changing attitudes to crime and its punishment with the introduction of trial by jury; the prevalence of drunkenness, poverty and prostitution; the growth of political nihilism etc. Another way (that of some Soviet critics of the 1920s) was to emphasise the melodrama at the expense of the philosophy - the extraordinary events, not the extraordinary ideas. Yet another way was to connect them all with *Notes from Underground* and the exploration of the problem of self-will - and by extension, the crucial problem of Freedom versus Authority. The fourth way - and the one which I will be concerned with for the rest of the talk - is to regard them consecutively as being a gradual disclosure of what he termed a 'new Christianity', culminating eventually in the characters of Alyosha Karamazov and Father Zosima in Dostoevsky's last novel.

Crime and Punishment was the first of the major post-Siberian novels. Its main theme is the murder by a young, impoverished, ex-student Raskolnikov of an evil old pawnbroker and her innocent sister, the psychological consequences of his crime, his friendship with a Christian prostitute Sonya, and his eventual decision to confess and to expiate his offence in Siberia in Sonya's company. The fundamental questions raised by Dostoevsky were: what were the motives for the crime, and what were its repercussions on the criminal both before and after his confession? Dostoevsky scholars writing from a committed Christian point of view have tended

---

[1] D.S.Mirsky, *A History of Russian Literature*, edited Francis J. Whitfield, 1949, p. 274

to see the novel - and I am generalising very broadly - as an illustration of the theme of guilt-suffering-expiation and regeneration. Such an approach lays much emphasis on Sonya's reading to Raskolnikov of the New Testament story of the raising of Lazarus from e dead, and on the Christian theme of redemption - if it is indeed redemption in Raskolnikov's case - with the novelty that the agent in the 'redemption process' is not a prostitute turned Christian, but a Christian driven by economic circumstances to prostitution. But is the process a convincing one, and is Raskolnikov redeemed? Certainly he is not repentant. He is not apparently regenerate (although there is some ambiguity about this, especially in English translations of the novel). He obstinately refuses to call what he did a crime, and leaves Sonya's copy of the New Testament unopened. The best that Dostoevsky can apparently offer in the epilogue is the hope of a slow, gradual regeneration in the future, which may, he says, form the subject of another story. But I think there may be an important conclusion to be drawn from what appears to be the inconclusive ending of the novel. Atonement for one's sins - suffering - is not the same thing as regeneration. It is not enough to confess one's guilt (whether or not one believes it *was* a crime), or to accept, even gladly to accept, the sentence of the law. That in itself is only a preliminary stage, necessitated in Raskolnikov's case by the need to overcome the terrible isolation from human beings which his action has caused. True regeneration Dostoevsky may be saying (as he himself believed) is something *outside one's own powers to achieve.* Raskolnikov by himself cannot achieve it, though he *can* confess and *can* suffer. Sonya may be able, through her love for him, to help him to achieve it. But beyond Sonya there is divine grace. Now, I do not myself believe that this is the major theme of *Crime and Punishment.* Raskolnikov does not believe in divine grace, and Sonya is hardly important enough to bear the whole burden of the Christian message. It seems to me that it is a negative point that Dostoevsky is establishing in *Crime and Punishment*, namely that left to his own devices man seems to arrive at a dead end. It is not so much a case of 'God's truth telling in the end'[1], as Dostoevsky said in a letter he wrote shortly before finishing the novel, outlining his intentions, but rather the negative proposition that man without God seems to come to grief.

Dostoevsky's next novel *The Idiot* takes his attempt to find an answer to Raskolnikov's dilemma a stage further. He said in a well-known letter to his niece that the main idea of the novel was 'to depict a positively good man'[2]; but that he feared for the success of his attempt because there was only one such man, namely Christ, and that

---

[1] Letter to M. Katkov, September, 1865, in *Dostevsky's Letters*, op. cit., Vol. 2, 1984, p. 175

[2] Letter to S. Ivanova, January, 1868, in *Dostoevsky's Letters*, op. cit. Vol. 3, 1990, p. 17, where the more literal translation 'positively beautiful person' is preferred.

writers who had tried to portray good figures in Christian literature - Cervantes and Don Quixote, Dickens and Mr Pickwick - only succeeded insofar as they made them comical or even ludicrous. In trying to create in Prince Myshkin, the idiot of the title, a positively good man, Dostoevsky clearly attributed to him certain Christ-like, or at least saintly features: his external appearance which bore resemblance to conventional portraits of Christ in Orthodox iconography (fair hair, sunken cheeks, thin, pointed, almost white beard, big, blue staring eyes); his simple, innocent, even childlike nature; his charitable acts; his kindness and consideration towards the underprivileged and victims of injustice; his love of children and animals; his meekness and submissiveness in turning the other cheek; his powers of foresight and divination; and his refusal to pass judgement on others.

At the same time Dostoevsky felt obliged in the interests of art to make Myshkin a complex and enigmatic figure; and in his notebooks for the novel he actually referred to the Prince as a Sphinx.[1] There is a deliberate duality in his character, perhaps even in his name Lev Myshkin (lion/mouse), and the thought did once cross my mind that Dostoevsky, in calling his Idiot by the Christian name and patronymic Lev Nikolaevich, was perhaps having a sly dig at that other Lev Nikolaevich - Tolstoy! He succumbs to what Dostoevsky calls 'double thoughts', and his normally trusting nature is at times soured by a certain gloomy, morbid suspiciousness and sense of alienation.

If Dostoevsky's conception of Christ played a part in the creation of his 'hero', there are also some features of Myshkin which reflect Dostoevsky's own situation and condition - his epilepsy; his absence from and return to Russia; his, at times, suspicious nature; his abnormally heightened awareness; or his outspoken views on Russia, the Russian people, the Russian Christ, or Catholicism as the begetter of socialism and atheism. Capital punishment seems to have had a fascination for Myshkin, and his reflections on the thoughts of a condemned man before his execution and his obsession with Holbein's picture of the crucified Christ taken down from the cross, which he fears might be a threat to Christian belief and that Christ might have died in vain - these are surely Dostoevsky's own.

It has been said, somewhat unfairly, that Dostoevsky, in 'creating Myshkin in his own and Jesus Christ's combined image, could not help mocking his own creation even as he sought to worship it'.[2] It is true that Myshkin comes to grief at the end of the novel, relapses into a state of idiocy and is seemingly destroyed beyond

[1] *The Notebooks for 'The Idiot'*, edited E. Wasiolek, translated K.Strelsky, 1967, p. 199.

[2] Ronald Hingley, *Dostoyevsky. His Life and Work,* 1978, p. 143.

human redemption. But perhaps this overlooks the fact that Christ was also destroyed beyond *human* redemption when he died on the cross. Is the ending yet another allusion to Christ the man, as opposed to Christ the Son of God? And is it not the case that unless one believed in the *divinity* of Christ, his life story on earth would also end in failure and humiliation?

This is not the place to weigh up the merits and defects of *The Idiot* as a novel. Its main character Prince Myshkin, however, is in my opinion a successful and artistically plausible portrait of an epileptic whose positive, saintly, even Christ-like attributes are balanced by his all too human weaknesses, but who is not the 'positively good man' whom Dostoevsky originally intended. Indeed one could argue that Dostoevsky was primarily concerned to show the ascendancy of evil over good in a world in which religious belief and the moral sanctions deriving from it have lost ground, and where the force of example is not sufficient to stem the tide of moral corruption and nihilism.

Dostoevsky's next novel *The Devils*, which takes its title from Luke's story of the Gadarene swine, is primarily a devastating attack on revolutionary nihilism, but problems of belief, doubt and unbelief are never far from sight. The complex central character, Stavrogin, is perhaps Dostoevsky's fullest embodiment of the principle of freedom without God, and like Svidrigailov in *Crime and Punishment* - a more ruthless exponent of the will to power than the more humane hero Raskolnikov - the only course left to him in the end is suicide. One of the minor characters, Kirillov, who has come under Stavrogin's spell, is a man with a profound thirst for religion and one who acknowledges Christ as the one being who gives meaning to life, but who cannot accept Christ's divinity. In his eyes Christ was murdered and the laws of nature did not spare even him - therefore the laws of nature must be evil. There can be no God; only an evil will. The argument follows the familiar lines that if there is a God, he must be evil to permit suffering; but if there is no God then everything is lawful. If there is no God then I am God and am bound to exert my own will. Raskolnikov had tried to do so by murdering a 'useless' old pawnbroker. But murder for Kirillov is the lowest form of the manifestation of self-will. For him, the highest manifestation is suicide, not to put an end to his own unhappiness, but to be a martyr in the cause of humanity!

Yet another minor character, Shatov, - also under Stavrogin's influence, but a different Stavrogin from the one who infected Kirillov, and who becomes the victim of a nihilist murder conspiracy, - is asked by Stavrogin the fundamental Dostoevsky question - do you believe in God? Shatov replies 'I believe in Russia, I believe in Orthodoxy, I believe in the body of Christ' - 'But in God?' continues Stavrogin.

And Shatov stammers in reply 'I...I...I will believe in God'.

Like Shatov, Dostoevsky was still tormented by doubt - doubt which was crystallised in Book 5 *Pro et Contra* of *The Brothers Karamazov,* which for many readers represents the high water mark of his artistic achievement, and which was to be answered, at least indirectly, in Book 6 *The Russian Monk.*

The crux of Book 5 is the conversation between two of the Karamazov brothers, Ivan, who can be seen in the context of the novel as representing Mind, and Alyosha, who may likewise symbolise Spirit, on the inevitable question of the existence of God. Ivan claims to accept God, but not his creation (that is to say the world). He accepts God, but immediately qualifies this by saying that the limitations of his own Euclidean mind don't allow him to be sure, that anyway it doesn't really matter and he may as well accept him as not. But he does know that the world exists, and he doesn't like it because of its cruelty and suffering. He then professes not to understand how one can love one's neighbour - it's just one's neighbour one can't love, he says - and then returns to his original point about suffering, above all the suffering of innocent children, and the cruelty of human beings which for him far exceeds the cruelty of animals. 'It's not God I don't accept', he concludes 'but I most respectfully return Him his ticket'. Alyosha calls this rebellion and reminds him of the one who can forgive and atone for the suffering of children, whereupon Ivan launches into his poem, as he calls it, about the 'One without sin and His blood', *The Legend of the Grand Inquisitor.* Set in 16th century Seville the Legend tells how Christ returned to earth, went round performing miracles, was arrested and imprisoned in the palace of the Holy Inquisition and sentenced by the Grand Inquisitor himself to be burnt at the stake. But first the Inquisitor interrogates Christ about the temptations in the wilderness, the three temptations which he says epitomised and foretold the whole subsequent history of mankind. For Christ's answers to them were the cause of all man's unhappiness. By refusing to turn stones into bread he failed to understand that one must first feed men before asking virtue of them. Christ gave them freedom, but denied them bread, but in the centuries since Christ men have said - make us your slaves, only feed us. There is no sin, only hunger.

Again, men want someone to worship. Give them bread, he says to Christ, and they will worship you. But you only gave them more freedom. Furthermore, you refused to cast yourself down from the pinnacle or to rule over the kingdoms of the world. You rejected the three powers which alone can hold men captive and make them happy - namely miracle, mystery and authority. In not succumbing to the temptations of the devil, you refused to enslave men by a miracle. But you asked too much of them. Only the elect could rise to the challenge. But did you come only for their sake? Whereupon the Inquisitor explains that he and the chosen few have corrected Christ's work and founded it on miracle, mystery and authority. We shall be Caesars, he says, to plan the universal happiness of mankind. We shall persuade men that they will only become free when they surrender their freedom to us. We shall tell them that every sin will be expiated if done with our permission; we will allow them to sin because we love them and we will take upon ourselves the punishment for their sins. Only we who guard the mystery will be unhappy. And that is why Christ must be burnt at the stake.

When the Inquisitor had finished, he waited for Christ to reply. But Christ made no reply. He merely kissed the old man on his lips. Whereupon the Inquisitor shuddered, opened the door and told Christ to go and never return.

Not surprisingly, Alyosha sees this as an unfair attack on the Roman Catholic Church; and it is perhaps no coincidence that Dostoevsky had been deeply disturbed by the declaration of papal infallibility a few years earlier. But Dostoevsky preferred to regard it as, in his opinion, the most powerful expression of atheistic ideas ever to have been penned in Europe, and said that he hoped to answer Ivan's blasphemy - though worried about his ability to do so - by the creation of the character of Father Zosima, the Russian Monk, in the book immediately following *Pro et Contra*. This book is made up of three parts:- Zosima's life story as a man of the world, his wise counsel and good deeds as a monk, and his so-called conversations and exhortations. The biographical notes about him record his progression from a fairly conventional childhood and youth and a wholesome home environment when he read his Bible regularly, by way of a drunken and debauched army life, the physical abuse of his manservant and an impending duel over a woman's honour, to a moment of truth, a refusal to fight, a plea for forgiveness and a retreat to a monastery. The chapters devoted to his teachings are Dostoevsky's attempt at a positive answer, if only an indirect one, to the atheistic propositions of Ivan and his Inquisitor. The essence of Zosima's philosophy is that the monastic life should be a preparation for going out into the world; that the monk is on the side of the people (*narod*); that salvation for Russia will come from the people because for all their sins they have God in their heart (are 'God-bearing'); that one must pray constantly; that one must love all God's creatures, animals and plants as well as humans; that hell is the suffering of being unable to love; and that above all *no-one* has the right to judge another, since we are all sinners and are all responsible to and for one another.

Book 6 was not of course intended to be a rational answer or a point by point refutation of the propositions advanced in Book 5. Dostoevsky's case rested partly on the force of example, and partly too on the direction in which the three Karamazov brothers appear to be moving as the novel ends. Ivan, the atheist or agnostic, is driven to confess to a crime he never committed and suffers brain fever. The sensual Dmitri, - symbol of Body, as Ivan and Alyosha symbolised Mind and Spirit, - having resisted the temptation to murder his hated father despite the easy opportunity to do so, readily accepts his 'guilt' and the harsh consequences of his wrongful conviction, because he knows in his heart that he had wished for his father's death, and gives his word before God to become a better man. Alyosha, whose innocence is threatened by the temptress Grushenka, comes through his temptation unharmed, and in the closing scenes apparently proclaims his faith in resurrection and the life to come.

This was not, however, intended to be Dostoevsky's final word. Had he lived, he had planned to take the brothers' subsequent fates a stage further. But as an artist he could never have reached an unequivocal conclusion, such that his readers could have said with certainty that he was on the side of Christ and not the Grand Inquisitor. As an artist he had to be ambiguous, to achieve balance, to pose problems, not solve them.Mikhail Bakhtin saw in Dostoevsky an author who created characters with points of view which would clash with the author's; whose voices would argue with the author's as well as with each other.[1] Dostoevsky made it clear in his correspondence that he completely shared Zosima's ideas, but that if it had been necessary to express them 'on his own behalf' (that is outside a work of fiction), he would have done so in a different form and a different language; and that his concern for the demands of art outweighed any inclination he might have had to point a moral.

But it was not *only* Dostoevsky's respect for his artistic conscience that made him unwilling to provide answers to the problems he had raised. Not far below the novel's surface lies that tension between doubt and belief which had plagued him all his life. As he wrote shortly before his death, echoing the words of the Devil in Ivan's nightmare: 'It's not as a *child* that I believe in Christ and profess him; *my* hosanna has passed through a great furnace of doubt'. Passed through, but not been entirely purged. And perhaps nothing could better articulate Dostoevsky's profession of faith than the words, so familiar to him, of the father of the boy possessed, in Mark's Gospel: 'Lord I believe. Help thou mine unbelief.'

---

[1] *Problems of Dostoevsky's Poetics*, edited and translated Caryl Emerson, 1984, passim.

VI   *Paul Valéry :   Of Things Divine*

– Paul P.-D. Gifford

The relations between literature and theology - between religion and culture generally - have always struck me as inexhaustibly fascinating. In America, the Modern Languages Association, at its annual congresses, regularly reserves a sectional meeting to research done in this area. We do not do so well in this country - possibly through a theological illiteracy characteristic of secular times, but more probably, I suspect, through a sort of British stiffness or inhibition that prevents us talking readily about things that are of deepest resonance to our authors, or ourselves; there is a sort of reserved zone, a no-go area.

Something of the same is true of Paul Valéry (1871-1945). *Of Things divine* is the title of a Socratic dialogue, in the manner of Plato, which Valéry conceived in 1921, but never finished and which was never published. If you had mentioned to any specialist of modern French literature up to ten years or so ago, that he might even have conceived such a thing, you would have been greeted rather like Nietzsche's prophetic madman. Valéry might be one of the most universal and incisive of all modern thinkers; he might be one of the most perfect poets of the century, one of the few minds to bridge the modern gulf between the cultures of art and of science, and many other admirable things things besides; but of any interest whatever in things divine, there appeared precious little evidence or prospect. The most settled conviction of all competent experts was that here was the purest son of the Enlightenment, successor to Descartes and Voltaire, intellectual factotum of the anticlerical Third Republic, a notorious adversary of that other great French mind whom he so much resembles in all things save in things divine, Pascal. An agnostic, a sceptic; not so much an irreligious man (though that too on occasion) - perhaps more an a-religious one, a 'modern'.

Then between 1957 and 1963 came the publication of the 28,000 pages of his notebooks, the experimental work devoted to the analysis of mind and the making of the products of mind - Valéry's real life's work as he himself saw it. The *Cahiers* are a seminal work unlike any other in the 20th century, infinitely more important than the published poetry, essays and drama which had brought Valéry fame in his lifetime. This was the submerged part of the iceberg. And as it came to be surveyed, what appeared to those who had eyes to see was that Valéry was, in that reserved space of his private notebooks, quite extraordinarily preoccupied with things divine. If the projected Socratic dialogue *peri ton tou theou* had not seen the light of day, it was certainly not for lack of sustaining interest. Quite the reverse: it was because the subject was too vast, too crucially important, and too delicate in its time. This, let us remember, is the period when religious matters in France are fiercely entangled with ideology and with politics; those of you who heard Malcolm Scott last year on the struggle for the soul of the novel between writers of the Catholic and Realist traditions[1] will have a strong sense of that important feature of the landscape. The subject was too close, as well, to the vital, spiritual nerve of his entire enterprise of the mind to be given away piecemeal, in publicly marketable bits. In Valéry's intellectual make-up there is a fierce Cathar-like integrity, an unswerving determination to think his own thoughts in his own way, authentically, and an extraordinary *pudeur*. 'To my mind', he says, 'it is an impurity to give to the most simple and secret part of ourselves an external definition and a name one hasn't oneself invented... My motto was: conceal your god' (C, VIII,611).[2] For all these reasons, the unfinished Dialogue had to go back to the central laboratory of his thought, back to the reserved space-time of the Notebooks.

And so Valéry's lifelong reflexion upon things divine is a private experiment. It is called, and rightly called, a Dialogue; but it stands in some ways in lieu of an exchange with living interlocutors that might have happenend but never really did. Why was this? Valéry was superbly connected: he knew a quite stunning array of writers, philosophers, scientists, musicians and mystics various, including all the leading lights of the French Catholic intelligentsia of his time - Claudel, Maritain, Teilhard de Chardin, Mauriac and the rest; his closest family by marriage were all believers committed in one of the Dominican lay orders. To explain why the Dialogue of things divine remains private, one has to understand two things of some importance in the century. One is the massive immobility of Catholic dogmatic orthodoxy between 1871 and 1945: here is a citadel religion dug in against the modern world, suspecting modernists and protestants under every rug, wedded to a philosophic system forged in 13th century. The other is the powerful, visceral rejection of the Catholic religious upbringing à l'ancienne mode which runs like a deep scar through so many artistic autobiographies of this period. To give some idea of the latter, I quote some barely disguised autobiographical reflections from some of Valéry's unpublished writings. The first one is semi humorous:

> When I was little, God seemed to me an extremely ingenious person who managed never to want what we wanted. He had a great role to play in

[1] See infra pp. 103 ff.

[2] References to Valéry's *Cahiers* given in the body of the text are to the in facsimile edition in XXIX volumes published by the CNRS (Paris, 1957-63).

illnesses and burials, you could feel his hand in all things, in everything people said. When it was fine, everyone was well and all went swimmingly, he disappeared into Churches that were kept gloomy on purpose so as to keep him in the dark. He was good, evil, absurd, highly ingenious, capable of anything and no getting away fom him. He always won in the end, which is boring to the mind and made him uninteresting. It seemed to me that I could come to an understanding with him if I wanted to and that he prevented me from wanting to. I didn't love him, not seeing how one could love so dangerous, strange, touchy, sharp-sighted a being...I counted on deceiving him in the end by being sincere through fear.[1]

The second is more acid-etched:

He spoke and <u>intoned</u>, as if tightrope-walking./ A voice so high-pitched that what it said was dangerously at risk - unbelievable! The tone of authority seemed to me an afterthought just as one might warm up yesterday's dinner. What they teach stands up only like a whipped-up top, it doesn't keep upright by itself. They whip up their truths with threats and promises...which give them power, value, ascendancy, but no intrinsic strength.[2]

In that intellectual resistance, dissociating the substance and form of things, one hears the first notes of the long, depreciatory hissing of the Valéryan Serpent in the Garden of Catholic sensibility and thought. This will be a favourite role of Valéry's, and an ambiguous one, since at the end of his famous poem 'A Serpent's Sketch', which is a parodic remake of the Genesis myth, Valéry has the Serpent claim - cheekily, but sincerely and perhaps even profoundly - that in reworking the poem of God's creation and in subverting the mother of humankind, he the Serpent has in fact acted for the greater glory of God.

However that may be, it is clear at least that there was little chance that the Serpent could really dialogue with the children of the Garden. Claudel said as much,[3] which is an impressive circumstance in itself, given that Claudel was a tireless converter

---

[1] Unpublished notebook 'Emma-Rachel' in *Histoires brisées* ms. III, t. f.4 verso. All Valéry manuscripts cited in this paper are kept at the Département des Manuscrits of the Bibliothèque Nationale, Paris.

[2] Ibid. f.6 verso

[3] While stressing his admiration for the poet Valéry, Claudel remarked:'As to the thinker, I consider he gets into a blind alley. I preferred never to become involved in discussion with him. It wouldn't have helped him or me. We would have tired each other out for nothing' (quoted by Robert Mallet in *André Gide Paul Valery, Correspondance*, Gallimard, 1955, p. 31).

who from his diplomatic post in China bombarded intellectual France with a stream of dialogues by correspondence. In thinking of Valéry he must have counted his stamp money and thought better of it! Even Teilhard, whom Valéry liked personally, whom he respected as an original seeker and with whom he did actually discuss on two or three occasions their respective ideas of things divine, draws from him these revealing comments. 'The delightful Teihard is dicing with his estate [as priest and as Jesuit]'(C,XVI,3); 'They [the intellectual priests] are trying to reach a new religious continent by swimming there' (C,XIV,716). That is an interesting image which supposes the notion of a shipwrecked orthodoxy, a notion that we shall indeed discover in Valéry's thought.

The chances of dialogue at home were not any better. Every one of Valéry's days was marked by the early morning departure for Mass of the three female members of his immediate family; so that his early morning work on the Notebooks - he used to get up at three or four o'clock in the morning to work, as he said, 'between the lamp and the sun' - constituted in effect a parallel and rival cult within the home. This religious divide within the family was entirely typical of Third Republic France. What is perhaps unusual and moving is the following exchange between husband and wife that I turned up in Valery's papers and was allowed by the family to divulge. It is entitled 'Morning preface that a wife asks a husband to read at the beginning of thought':

> O Christ, when when I try for a moment to envisage you as God, you are an enigma to me. My mind cannot tolerate you...If you are the light of the world (you have said so) illuminate an intelligence that does not understand you and would think to destroy itself in admitting you. You are called way and truth. Give me the desire to know them. May I not refuse to make a beginning in pursuit of them and to ask this of you. And you, do not refuse then to hear me.

To which the husband replies:

> I cannot think that light is in two opposing states. If one of these demands contradictions, essential obscurities in indefinite number, refusal of observation and proof, useless cruelties, the receiving of propositions that are declared to be incomprehensible and which fulfil no function in thought; the negation of other propositions which, rigorously and reasonably drawn from analyses and observations, have no other defect than that they contradict affirmations unproven and unsustained etc - is it not our duty to prefer the other light? And how can the intelligence do other than prefer itself, its own

tendency and increase in its own ways - and prefer these things above all to that way which appears to it only in the moment when it despairs of itself and its co-ordinate act - and turns towards the vague resource, the feeling that dies away if it is clarified - the very shadow of itself.[6]

There is a lot one could say by way of commentary on that exchange which highlights better than any I know the relation between religion and culture, the one light and the other, at a certain place in a certain time (the year is 1913). But of course it speaks pretty well for itself; and it says among other things that there could be no exteriorised dialogue, not even within the intimacy of marriage. No, in its time, Valéry's reflection had to be a closed-circuit monodialogue of thought.

But why should it have been even that? What is it that puts things divine on Valéry's intellectual agenda in the first place and keeps them there so insistently? Perhaps most profoundly the need to address a wound of the understanding, a wound fresh and potent in Valéry's time and still largely unhealed in our own. I refer to that traumatic event in European culture - that sea-change of consciousness, that shipwreck, that eclipse - which is generally known by the shorthand name Nieztsche gave to it, the Death of God. 'Shipwreck' is the title of a poem, highly uncharacteristic in tone and manner, that Valéry wrote in 1909, having just completed his reading on the one hand, of the complete works of Nietzsche (he reviewed these for the *Mercure de France* as they appeared in their French translation by Henri Albert), on the other hand, of the works of Saint John of the Cross, discovered by chance in a library. One might predict that between those two poles some kind of spark would leap. And so it does:

> What hour is this that shudders 'gainst the hull,
> What squall of darkness, dislocating fate,
> What power impalpable rattles in the rigging
> The skeleton bones of all our deaths?
>
> I see the Christ lashed to the mast
> Dancing to death and foundering with his own;
> His bloody eye illuminates the scripture writ
> A GREAT SHIP HAS PERISHED WITH ALL HANDS.[2]

---

[1] Loose-leaf manuscript attached to *Cahier* L-13 of the original series, BN

[2] 'Sinistre' was published in the 1942 edition of the *Poésies* (Gallimard), but figures in the *Oeuvres* (ed. Hytier, Pleiade, Gallimard, t. I. 1957) only in the section"Mélange", p. 301. Valéry himself disliked it and left it aside from the *Album des vers anciens* in 1920.

Now for a subtle Symbolist poet, that is fairly crude stuff; it <u>sounds</u> as if Valéry has been swallowing a lot of neat Nietzsche, possibly laced with a reminiscence of Wagner's *Flying Dutchman* too. But the message at least is not new: Valéry's own voice had said something very similar more than twenty years earlier. In 1888, as a 17 year-old schoolboy never having read Nietzsche, he wrote a prose poem in which the young narrator, as if in a dream, witnesses a funeral, which, he is told, is that of God. There follows a cosmic cataclysm:

> Then it was that the sun, after a last brightness, paled and disappeared. Something warned me it would not return and that we should not see it more.The moon itself had melted in the skies. The dark firmament held no more stars. It was a cold dark hole. And at that moment I felt falling on to my hands from above a few icy drops like melting diamonds and I understood that all the stars had come loose and that I was witnessing the tears of heaven flow.

> A great cry rent the air. A great wind stirred up the leaves that covered the earth..And it seemed to me that this wind blew within me and extinguished my Being.[1]

That is much better writing, extraordinarily impressive in fact for a 17-year old, with its powerful symbolism of eclipse and apocalyptic disorder, its bold and subtle correspondences of inner and outer worlds; though if pressed, I might still be inclined to detect a hyperbole of the Romantic heart, and a form of pathetic fallacy, behind this presentation of an event in culture as an event in nature.

That Romantic hyperbole seems to me quite inseparable, however, from the whole notion of a Death of God. This expression, it appears to me, is not to be taken quite literally; indeed it is, in a literal sense, incoherent - or very nearly. The sense of the term God, in any recognisable acceptance, certainly excludes the idea that God at one time was but has now suffered decease. There are only two ways you can make 'God is dead, we have killed him' into a statement which makes sense as a metaphysical assertion: one is to suggest that God was only ever a human idea anyway, which is what I take Nietzsche to be saying; and that is the atheistic understanding followed by many in 20th century. The other is to suggest that God did historically die, killed by men, but is not deceased in the metaphysiscal sense claimed. That is of course the very singular affirmation of Christianity, the doctrine of Cross and Resurrection. Otherwise, the only possible meaning attaching to the

---

[1] This unpublished prose poem figures in the dossier *Proses anciennes* f. 115-16, BN

phrase is an anthropological one, describing a form of consciousness, the mentality and outlook of a given culture at a given time. A particular idea or set of ideas of God, or perhaps the category as such of a God - the 'theistic hypothesis' - has, as we say, 'gone dead on us'. That is an entirely coherent sense, and a very important one - quite as awesome, indeed, as Valéry suggests when he equates it to the loss of the sun of Being, or presents it as the shipwreck of a culture.

This latter sense, the metaphysically agnostic one, is Valéry's sense. He was too immediately aware of the genesis in mind of all ideas to follow Nietzsche's lyrical leap into atheism: what man has been able to kill off is likely to be, not the ultimate metaphysical principle of things, if such there be, but rather a god-idea and an alienating form of the religious relationship. 'I do not say', he writes, 'that there is no God. I say, before saying whether there is or is not a god, I must ask myself what such and such a reply would mean in me. / It is the question [or demand] that I must first examine, to see if I truly understand it - if I would have created it on my own account, or if I am simply reproducing it' (C, XVIII, 481). Valéry shows himself here as a sceptic in the original Greek sense - <u>skeptikos,</u> one who examines. His idea is to take back the entire nexus of questions and problems that make up the science of things divine into the psychological and human sphere, to replace it within the universe of mind-made meanings and values. He proposes to ask how thought about divine things comes to be generated in our minds; what the religious function of the human psyche is and how it works; he wants to rethink the whole process by which we ask religious questions and verify the legitimacy of the answers - are they intelligible, coherent, necessary? are they or not divine? What is this value-category of 'the divine' we carry about with us? Can we do without it? What can we actually do with it for the greatest development of human potential?

The last question is not just a matter of disinterested psycho-philosophical enquiry; it is, as Valéry was very sharply aware, a vital existential question about the fulfilment of his own spiritual nature, his own need for transcendence - and mankind's too. It is a very striking fact about Valéry and many others of his generation that the death of God is, though deeply traumatic, a galvanising, and a creative trauma: as the great Explicator-Respondent of the Western soul is lost to philosophic view and to the assurance of faith, so the question of what to do with man, particularly higher, spiritual man acquires an anguished prominence. Thus, in Valéry's poem 'Poésie', the soul who has known ecstatic communion at the source of Being, thought of as maternal, is now thrust out from that intimacy and speaks in anxious reproach: 'What shall I be without love?'. That is not the same question as in St Paul's letter to the Corinthians, though the echo is no doubt a conscious one. It means 'What shall I be without providential care?'; and even more, it means:

'what will become of my upreaching, my *eros* henceforth devoid of any ultimate Object of its aspiring?'. That is the key question; and it gives tremendous point and urgency to Valéry's attempt to convert his examination of the god-function in Psyche into an art of 're-inventing the divine'.

Valéry has, vaguely enough - this is a positivist assumption inherited from Auguste Comte and not uncommon in France at the turn of the century - the idea that from a sufficiently subtle and rigorous study of this function of the human psyche, one might be able, in the absence of any knowledge of the Absolute as such, to reinvent a god-idea that will be serviceable to man. Equally, he has - but here with deep longing and powerfully focussed intent - the desire to derive from the same study a parallel and rival construct of spirituality, a 'mysticism without God', as he calls it, which will be a viable personal rsponse to the soul's question. It is here, perhaps, in this dialogue between the resolve to re-examine the religious function in man and the need to re-invent the form of its intentional movement, that one senses the the dynamism and the inexhaustible fascination for Valéry of his long Odyssey of research concerning the things divine.

It is indeed an Odyssey, one of the greatest of the century. It leads him to rethink all the forms of 'transcendental' thought that have traditionally formed the framework of our Western culture. It has many interlocutors: the great metaphysicians of rationalist Europe, the mystics, the Christian gospels, the believers and the unbelievers of common coinage. It has its intercessors too and its adversary angels: Mallarmé, Descartes and Goethe, among the first; Pascal, St John of the Cross and Nietzsche among the second. It embraced everything Valéry wrote and took more than 50 years. All I can offer here is the merest glimpse of a few significant patterns that emerge and perhaps some sense of the total figure.

I want to concentrate, as the framework of these lectures invites me to do, on Valéry's relations with Christian theology. But it is crucial to stress at the outset that this emphasis is, in certain important senses, foreign to Valéry's own natural movement of thought. In the first place, Christian theology is by no means the primary object, statistically or chronologically speaking, of Valéry's critique; it only comes into prominence relatively late, obliquely, almost as a kind of afterthought. The rationalist impulse from the Enlightenment through to various forms of deconstructionism in our own time is to insist on a 'level playing field of thought', and therefore to bracket and set aside any particularity, especially a particular dogmatic orthodoxy, above all one that looms large by its traditional prestige, its social position or its affective hold on the religious imagination within our culture. One of the things the so-called 'Death of God' does is to create the climate in which it becomes natural to think of Christianity as a standard exemplar of a generic type of psychic product - "metaphysics and religions", as Valéry often calls them.

There are no doubt gains involved in this generic approach: one of them is to foreground the simple but immensely significant fact that the god-idea most of us live with most of the time is not, in fact, made up of notions derived with pristine accuracy or deepest insight from the horse's mouth of Christian theology at all (even supposing, which is a condition not realised in Valéry's experience, that the discourse of Christian theology has the grace of prophetic depth, insight, and faithfulness). Rather, they are spontaneous inventions of the religious imagination, heavily conditioned by a variety of cultural inputs. For instance, in one of his early notebooks, Valéry simply lists the attributes of the current or common notion of God: 'God - the Creator and Knower/The public protector / The all-powerful and indestructible self / The Judge and Avenger / The Indecipherable / The being of Contradictions always future and imminent, hidden and about to reveal himself. Enigma. Demand. Man (vir) amplified - Zeus/ Sensibility and intellect amplified / Universal law <u>as it is</u>/ Limit-unity of the universe'(C, IV, 86). There is the composite God-image of his time. The words Creator, Judge, and perhaps the word 'sensibility' indicate some form of Christian imprint or tincture; but the rest suggests Romantic longing and mathematical idealism, spiritualism, esoterism, social utilitarianism, Wagner - a whole brew of 19th century thought forms.

Indeed, if I were pressed to say what the <u>primary</u> object of Valéry's deconstructive <u>critique</u> of religious thought forms is, I would be tempted to reply: the 19th century imagination of transcendence. In a highly significant note, Valéry calls himself 'the metaphysical Michelson'.[1] He means by that that he sees himself repeating in the domain of mind, of mind-made values and meanings, the experiment of evacuation conducted in the realm of physics by Michelson and Morley, an experiment disproving the hypothesis that there exists a universal fluid medium 'ether' capable of explaining the transmission at a distance of electro-magnetic forces. Centrally, Valéry is concerned to bale the spiritualist ether out of Psyche.

Here one may ask the more radical question: is it certain that Christian doctrine can ever be a pure essence distilled out of, standing independently from, a culturally conditioned language of thought? Should not the religion of Incarnation accept this condition as a sign of the necessary imperfection of its theological discourse - there

---

[1] For this role model in Valéry's thought, see chap. 2 of my *Valéry, le Dialogue des choses divines,* Paris, Corti, 1989

is no revealed <u>theology</u> - and of its need for constant renewal? Another profoundly suggestive note in the Cahiers says: 'What an extraordinary marriage between Aristotle and Plato, the Jewish Scriptures and St Paul wrought by the W. Middle-Ages. It is the mixture, the combination that was so important for Europe' (C, XI,110). It is true, particularly in Continental countries, that Christianity has been expressed intellectually in the terms and categories inherited from Greek metaphysics. One of the most significant things happening in the cultural sea-change of the end of the 19th century is that this particular synthesis of reason and revelation comes undone, so that intellect and faith are left looking at each other, not in complementarity and mutual support, but now in hostility and critical incomprehension.

This is very clear in Valéry's analysis of the metaphysics of religion. The constant thrust of his psychopoetics in this area is to ask whether our metaphysical assertions are not born of the mind's impotence in resolving the problems posed by our enquiring sensibility and created by the interrogative forms of our language. So he notes for instance:' "God" considered as name and figure of being given to whatever man cannot manage to determine - that which he feels to be above all else - he who cannot specify except in detail, fragmentarily ...'(C, V, 279). And again:'God or the geometric convergence at the infinite of our instincts. He's a mathematical symbol - allows us to write - - Propositions into which this noun enters. Being. That by which something exists when you are asleep, when you were not, when you will no longer be...You can only explain what is by what, strictly speaking, is not. Everything happens as if...Imaginary closure of things cf. the self. An infinite somebody. The self and the god. Generalised self' (C, IX, 235). So the god-idea is seen here as an epistemological symbol born of the need to explain and to render the unknown reciprocal to thought.

Within that frame of psychogenetic explanation, Valéry tries to understand the metaphysical self or soul. This, he says, is 'an essentially dualist and Christian idea' (along with the oppositions good and evil, nature and supernature): 'The Greeks didn't manage to separate the body from the soul to the same extent as the Christians a few centuries later. So that one can, one must regard the Christian soul as the result of a more recently invented operation. <u>Psyche</u> (Gr.) is like <u>anima</u> - the breath >= the sign of life >= sensibilty and potential activity that can be taken away from a being >= therefore separable from it >= consequently separable from what is observed to be corruptible, destructible >= therefore indestructible, incorruptible' (C,XIII, 712). Now, there is no doubt that the Christian notion of the soul has often received a strongly dualistic formulation in historically attested forms of Christian spirituality and culture. Valéry is not alone in thinking this: Bertrand Russell, for instance, goes much further in treating the soul as evidence of a form of Christian dualism.[1] And yet, I am sure that St Mary's College here is the place if anywhere to say that this is a delicate and crucial misunderstanding. It arises precisely from this characteristically early 20th century move of bracketing the particularity of the Judaeo-Christian tradition. The 'more recently invented concept' really cannot be explained, as the Greek psyche might be, as a notion engendered by the sense of a discrepancy between the sensation of vital energy, on the one hand, and the evidence of bodily mortality, on the other. It has its roots, surely, in Jewish thought, which is not rationalistic and is so little spiritualistic, philosophically speaking, that it developed only very late a doctrine of personal immortality (not indeed as a rational deduction or speculation but as an act of faith in the sovereign power of the Creator God who purposes the redemption and exaltation of the whole of the created world - who indeed creates anew). In the founding Christian event, that logic is powerfully developed. If the eternal Son becomes incarnate, lives and dies in the most material flesh, is raised by God in a form that preserves with that same flesh a mysterious but certain relationship, then one is obliged in all logic to say that that is the end of dualism in any ultimate sense; dualism is abolished in the principle of its possibility. After that, the immortality of the soul is really neither here nor there. One has to believe, as the Church has done, when it has been mindful of its own proper logic, in the Resurrection of the body (or 'the flesh') and the life everlasting.

Now we might ask our theological colleagues to say how far all this was common ground in Christian discourse of Valéry's generation. Reinhold Niebuhr, for one, who was of course Protestant, tells us that the ordinands of his time had the greatest trouble in subscribing to that article of the Apostles' Creed I have just mentioned. Describing the reversal of attitudes that came in subsequently during his lifetime he states: 'There is no part of the Apostolic Creed which, in our present opinion, expresses the whole genius of the Christian faith more neatly than just that despised phrase "I believe in the Resurrection of the body"'.[2] The interesting thing is that Valéry saw that point much sooner than the ordained minister. He says roundly: 'The Church is ashamed of its principal dogma, namely the Resurrection. Christianity can be summarised in two words: Christ is risen, he will raise us. But of this there is no mention. The immortality of the soul has little by little veiled, absorbed the Resurrection. The inconceivable has appeared more avowable, more distinguished, more true than the conceivable' (C, VI, 258). Does Valéry then conceive the resurrection of the body? Well, nearly: you would need to start, he says, from a materialist image of life and then envisage a reconstitution of the bodily edifice 'by infraction to Carnot'(C, XV, 41): that is, by a reversal of the principle of entropy, the

---

[1] See *Religion and Science*, London, Butterworth, 1935, p. 116 and passim

[2] *Beyond Tragedy. Essays on the Christian Interpretation of History*, London, Nisbet, 1938, pp. 289-290

thermodynamic principle which describes universal energy loss in isolated systems and the disorganisation of their forms. And as someone who had studied St Thomas, Valéry could and did think that hypothesis thinkable - although he adds,'infinitely unlikely'.

His critique of the notion of the soul is an interesting case: it displays in miniature the Greek and Judaeo-Christian elements of our cultural synthesis clearly, and the crisis that results from their coming apart. It perhaps suggests also that the outcome of the psychogenetic deconstruction practised by Valéry and a whole line of French thinkers after him is not, as many of one's professional colleagues casually assume - not least in France itself - hostile in practical effect to Christian theology. It may indeed have the effect of sifting the gold out of the cultural silt and discovering precisely that region of authentic human concern to which a theology knowing its business would wish to speak. If we had time, that contention could be tested in respect of other elements of Valéry's critique of religious metaphysics, for instance of the received notions of creation, or finality or even of evil.

To be sure, Valéry's analysis does not always explicitly acknowledge as its necessary complement a Christian theological understanding. His view of evil, to take that single example, is very markedly a relativistic, post-Kantian, post-Enlightenment view, mortal to all theodicies. Only once does Valéry the psychopoetician and anti-theodicist have a distant intimation of his theological complement. It comes when, celebrating at the Sorbonne at the very end of his life the 250th anniversary of the birth of Voltaire, Valéry imagines the great 18th century scourge of human crime and wickedness revisiting the modern world and reviewing the appalling destruction wrought by the Second World War. He concludes boldly and brilliantly, by having Voltaire use the words of the crucified Christ, 'They know not what they do'.[1] Admittedly, those words are shorn of their gospel preface, 'Father, forgive them'; but then that is perhaps the point of complementarity. It may be that what cannot be derived from the inspection of the mirror of Psyche is precisely the notion of the fatherhood and the forgiveness of God and the relation of these things to the problem of evil.

It should be clear from this preliminary look at his deconstruction of theistic metaphysics that Valéry perceives Christianity primarily as a system of the world. 'Le christianisme' is for him an -ism, an ideology. As such, he sees it as methodically cancelling out our unknowing about everything ultimate in the human condition, of having an answer to everything: 'How can one believe..this would be to have an

---

[1] 'Voltaire', p. 530, in *Oeuvres* (ed. Hytier, t.1, 1957)

answer to everything'(C, X, 701). That identification may seem strange perhaps to students of this time and place; and if so, that is all to the good, because it would indicate that the 20th century has on the whole learned to know the difference between an ideology (as in the expression 'a dead ideology') and a religious faith (we speak of 'a living faith'). But we must appreciate that such an identification was entirely comprehensible in neo-Thomist, post-Vatican I France, where theology did mean authorised and authoritative onto-theology. About this form of mind, Valéry says essentially that it kills the religious nerve by the Answer once and for all given, whereas it is the infinity of the Question, forever exceeding any available answer, that constitutes the dynamic of <u>homo</u> <u>transcendens</u>. Valéry even extended that notion of the misdemeaning Answer, again comprehensibly enough - though here I believe mistakenly - to the Christian notion of revelation as such. 'Why do you blaspheme the name of the Lord?/ Because... I can. Why has he a name?' (C, XX, 209). God is deniable when named, that is to say, when defined and limited; and our naming limits us spiritually.

Secondly, Christianity is for Valéry a religion. In this respect, he often speaks of Catholic Christianity, at least, with awe and a sort of deeply nostalgic tenderness: it is 'the most experienced, the cleverest, the most truly profound religion there has ever been' (C,VII, 868). That judgement combines deep aesthetic appreciation for the Catholic liturgy - even the mighty Mallarmé and the divine Richard Wagner were, in Valéry's eyes, mere imitators of the one great drama of the Mass[1] - with an admiration for its psychological and political virtue as an organising principle in human affairs. But he is clear that however beautiful it may be, whatever the profound and subtle human wisdom of its construction, the House is uninhabitable. Hume and Kant have knocked away the philosophic underpinning in natural theology, the so-called 'theistic proofs'. Reflexive knowledge of the processes of imagination and desire - much more cogent for Valéry than German text criticism - has revealed the fragility of the tradition and of the historical foundations. 'How are we supposed to believe in respect of things invisible men whom we see so ill or naively instructed of visible things? They describe archangels and know nothing of microbes..they know what happens to you after death but not in what life consists. Moreover, the knowledge they lack is no impediment to the the knowledge they claim to possess....'(C, XVIII, 745). 'Religion is unfortunately founded on historical facts of very distant antiquity, the most important of which are of almost zero

---

[1] In a letter of Sept. 1891 to Gide, Valéry writes: 'I don't want to go on about it - you are already saying I'm long-winded - but this would need to be said and shouted out loud: we are all little boys, beside the liturgists and the theologians, since the greatest geniuses among us, Wagner, Mallarmé, bow down and Imitate (*Corr. Gide-Valéry*, p. 126).

probability' (C, XVII, 431)...'God has wanted to make himself known to us by the least sure of ways. He communicates himself only through history. He did not confide himself to physics' (C, VII, 141). 'God has preferred to cause his only son to perish than speak to us clearly and incontestably' (C, VI, 415). As you can perhaps begin to hear in these last quotations there is in Valéry a kind of knot of exasperated fury and resentment at Christian incomprehensibility.

There is something more adversarial still in his relation to Christianity. This has to do with the third and crucial aspect in which he perceives it: as a presentation or representation of the divine. Is there anything in Christianity which is divine? For Valery, most of the things that might establish its claim in this regard are negatively weighted, following Nietzsche. The organising intuition of his critique is as follows: 'The capital act of the gospel has been the introduction of emotional sensibility into "religion". A truly extraordinary invention, with god, death, fellow humans, love - to have made a novel and heady brew of all that, a mixture of terror and hope, exaltation and abasement, excitement and simulation of feelings' (C, XVII,289). In other words, Christianity is seen as the perfectly anthropomorphic religion, the religion of the person-God symmetrical to the all-too-human person of man. 'Of the divine. The god of the Christians, too moralistic, too emotional, too pleasure-and-pain, excluding the constructive activity of man. The maximum maximorum is him, is therefore pre-established; the greatest efforts can attain no other perfection' (C, VI, 434). 'I judge a religion on the importance it gives to man, to the "destiny" of the individual, to his feelings, his acts, his value. The greater the importance it gives us, the smaller the importance I attach to it. The divine being that by which man detaches himself from himself, tends to count himself as nothing to obtain one of his joys or to consider himself as a thing among things - is thus the opposite of a god who takes account of man...'(C, VIII, 724)

The Person-God, or the inexplicable divine need of a human Other; the all-too-human person, and its need of a metaphysical Other. This unholy commerce of needs and interests establishes the Christian religion in Valéry's eyes as the ultimate idolatry. It is, of course in the name of this same suspicion of the anthropomorphic principle that Valéry undertakes to fit Christianity into the same formula by which he he accounts for all other natural i.e. purely human religions - the formula of mental parthenogenesis, the autonomous creation by the human mind of the religious poem destined to make good its essential deficit or lack. On this account, Christianity is the last, but also the most sophisticated and successful of the mythical Complements engendered by man's metaphysically desiring sensibility. Divine love itself, on this view, is a late correction to the primitive poem of religious humanity. 'Faith is born often of fright, prayer from fear - and the first demand of religion is to fear God...That is why love was introduced very late into the system. It was necessary to enhance God, and make him divine' (C, XXV, 415).

The same principle of explanation informs Valéry's critical christology, which is perhaps the ultimate form taken by his attempt to establish the psychogenetic formula of the Christian religion. From turn-of-the-century Catholicism, Valéry picks up the - surely awful? - expression 'l'Homme-Dieu, the Man-God'. His procedure, simply put, is to show that the Jesus of the gospels is neither truly man nor truly God. Is he God? But then why no scientific omniscience? How can his sufferings be taken seriously? How can one identify with a Redeemer without sin? But, on the other hand, is he even man? 'There is against the Man-God this grave objection that a two-fold experience and a two-fold example are lacking in his story. No sexual life. No intellectual life. Two problems not even enunciated. Alongside that, the most mediocre temptations, so mediocre that the devil is forever dishonoured. But there should have been all temptations and in all their force. The divine solutions of these signal temptations. That is what is lacking and surprisingly lacking in the gospel. Man there is not all that man is. Nor the devil' (C, XXVIII, 57).

I must leave to better endowed minds than mine the substantial points about the lack of a sexual and of an intellectual life in the gospel portrait of the exemplary Human Being, the Son of Man: they do indeed need to be enunciated, other than by the Scorceses of this world. All I can manage here, as a mere literary man on a theological excursion ticket, is the devil. Actually, he is the easier part of the proposition, being himself something of a littérateur. It is clear from other notes why Valéry thought the gospel temptations so mediocre. What he read in St Matthew's account of this episode was the offer of 'all the kingdoms of the earth and their glory', and this he interpreted to mean the offer made to the putative Son of God to become a large-scale landowner! My knowledge of Valéry's system of references convinces me that this is almost certainly a case of imaginary crossed wires: Valéry is projecting on to the gospel narrative a sense derived from the last act of Goethe's Faust, which he was re-reading at the same time: Faust, you will remember, is tempted to find a sufficient satisfaction of his immortal longing in the work of reclaiming lands from the sea. Valéry probably read the other temptations with the same mythically-charged literalism: the invitation to transform the stones into bread would mean the temptation of a good blow-out; throwing oneself from the temple roof the incitement to magic flight - both motifs, incidentally, also associated with the Faust myth, but signally transcended, it seems to me, in the gospel, which has to do with resisting the single diabolical temptation, that of trying to make oneself god through the exercise of power in its different forms. I suspect that colleagues in St Mary's, pondering this spectacular misreading by Valéry, might very reasonably incriminate his cavalier disregard for textual criticism and hermeneutics, a science which Valéry once dismissed - this word too is of its time - as 'une niaiserie protestante' ('a bit of Protestant nonsense') (C, XXV, 592).

Where does this critical christology lead? It leads back to Valéry's founding axiom 'That the Man-God has not happpened' (C, XXVIII, 57) and it points forward to the vertiginous opportunity, the formidable responsibility also, of ensuring that the divine should occur instead through the development of human potential itself. Valéry of course, together with the whole Nietzschean generation, has his variation on the theme of the Superman, the self-creator. He even falls out rather spectacularly with Nietzsche about how he is to be conceived[1]. There is however a difference: in Valery's case, self-creation remains an eminently religious activity, a consciously espoused form of mysticism, albeit an unbelieving one. It is in a true sense a dark night of the soul, with its own principle of desire waiting in purity upon an essentially needful and yet essentially deniable Absence. 'If you will, O my Reason, I will say, you will let me say, that my soul, which is yours also, felt itself to be the hollow form of a jewel casket, or the hollow of a mould and this void felt itself to be awaiting an admirable object - a sort of material spouse such as could not exist - for this divine form, this utter absence, this Being that was but Non-Being and the Being of what cannot Be - required an impossible matter, and the living hollow of this form knew that such material substance - was lacking and would forever be lacking from the world of bodies and their acts' (C, XXV, 618-19).

Valéry the pure, we might be tempted to say in conclusion, Valéry the Cathar; Valéry or the impossible Incarnation of the divine. And we would be right - or nearly so. Because the very last words of Valéry's 28,000 page Odyssey, scrawled in trembling pencil in the last of the notebooks, do actually read: 'The word love has been associated with the name of God only since Christ' (C, XXIX, 911). It would take longer than I have to say how those words came to be there and why they mark a 'Turning point'. And though there is a good chance that a severe specialist of comparative religion might find fault with the propositional sense offered by Valéry's last trace, there is no doubt in my mind that it has essentially a commissive value; and that what it means, among other things, is that the Serpent did, after all, wager that he had operated, albeit in opposition, for the greater glory of God.

---

[1] The private notes of 1909 adopt a fiercely critical attitude to Nietzsche whom Valéry found 'specious', 'lyrically inflated', 'a stimulus rather than a nourishment'. The following extracts offer some idea of this reaction of Apollo to Dionysos and suggest Valéry's rival project of anti-religious revolt: 'Nietzsche = Wagner. As if music were true'(f.129); 'Nietzsche, the least scientific of men, the most likely to poison you with morality' (f.128); 'Not classic, like all protestants' (f.109); 'Not Mediterranean. Not Greek, not Roman, no organising sense' (f.112); 'The subterranean theme of the priest' (f.120); 'He wants to improve man: protests against the corruption of humanity. He believes in a nature to be exalted and a counter-nature to be scorned. He has no critical sense./Whereas all history shows, if it shows anything - that Christians have never been christian...' (f.112); 'Why this war against the Ideal, when it is enough - and this is the modern duty! - to reduce it to what it is - an idea. It is enough to describe it minutely to strip it of any magic virtue - then it breaks down into ill-determined representations' (f.ll9); 'Christian, all too Christian' (f.ll9); 'Imitation of Jesus Christ'(f. 128);'How is it that this capital question - of pride - is not explored critically?' (f.122, verso). Dossier *Philosophie* I, BN.

VII   *Against the Tide:*
The Christian Novelist in the French Mainstream

– Malcolm Scott

(Note: The translations of French quotations in the text are the author's; the original texts are cited in the footnotes)

Theology and literature are often seen as unlikely bed-fellows, at best turning their backs on each other in mutual indifference, at worst incompatible to the point of divorce. Louis Veuillot, that sharp-minded French Second Empire polemicist, comes right to the point as he always did: 'The Christian feels the need to thicken and multiply veils, the artist the need to tear them open.'[1] The image is an arresting one, opposing theology's defence of dogma to the interrogative and iconoclastic spirit of literature, which at its best challenges old values and creates new ones. The 'received' ideas which Gustave Flaubert lists in his *Dictionnaire des idées reçues* and against which he brought all his powers of irony to bear include the 'revealed truths' of traditional religion. 'All so-called revealed truth', declared Emile Zola around the same time, 'is a lie'.[2] The artist's mode of 'revelation' was seen as being of a different order. Veuillot's image of him removing veils to show us what lies beneath would seem to make the writer the accomplice less of Saint John the Divine than of Salome.

The artist as he who daringly uncovers the naked truth is already present in another form a century and a half earlier, in a pioneering work of French fiction, *Le Diable boiteux*, by Lesage. In this novel, the limping devil of the title guides a reluctant tourist around the streets of Madrid, lifting the roofs off houses as he goes and inviting him to peer inside at the intimate scenes of domestic life. Charles Dickens, in *The Old Curiosity Shop*,[3] identifies this Cook's tour with a difference as an image of the novelist's relationship with his public, and as a metaphor for the process of artistic revelation, the disrobing of reality which was the *raison d'être* of the novel. That Lesage should entrust this role to a devil, and that he should give to this devil the name of Asmodée or Asmodeus, the demon lover from the Apocryphal Book of Tobit, and whose name means 'the Destroyer', betrays the novelist's awareness of the diabolically subversive nature of his art. We can read a lot into the fact that

---

[1] J. Barbey d'Aurevilly, *Oeuvres romanesques complètes*, Bibliotheque de la Pléiade, 1964-66, vol. I, p. 1300

[2] In his last novel *Vérité*, the culmination of his decades-long challenge to Catholic doctrine.

[3] C. Dickens, *The Old Curiosity Shop*, Harmondsworth, Penguin Books, p. 319

the most famous of modern French Christian writers, François Mauriac, also saw the action of 'lifting the roofs off houses' as an emblem of his own art: and that his most successful play is given the title *Asmodée*.

The notion that the novel is the province of the devil reappears in the work of Julien Green, the French novelist of American parentage, who claims to feel the presence of Satan in the moment of writing. The novelist, says Green, offers Satan an expansion of his kingdom through the effect of his work on his readers. Green himself, though convinced of the truth of Christianity, saw the novel as so profane and so dangerous a genre that he consciously avoided religious themes until he was nearing his sixtieth year. As for Mauriac, who had read Freud as well as Saint Augustine, fictional characters expressed the novelist's repressed instincts, and, he added provocatively, the more his own characters asserted themselves against any moralising intention he might have in creating them, the better the novel. However, like Green, Mauriac genuinely wondered what effect his novels would have on readers.[1] In his essay *Dieu et Mammon* he pondered whether he should not give up writing novels: as a Catholic he was obliged to hate sin, and as a novelist impelled to imagine it. But, he concluded with the aid of the philosopher Jacques Maritain, a good tree cannot bring forth evil fruit; purify the source![2] Some date Mauriac's decline as a novelist from this decision. Certainly, in the last thirty-five years of his long life, he was more successful as a journalist and political commentator; though, when I went to visit him just a few years before his death, I found him still haunted by his image as a novelist. Nobel Prize-winner or not, to many fellow Catholics he was, in his words, 'Public Enemy Number One'.

The same dilemma had been faced before Mauriac by the nineteenth-century writer Jules-Amédée Barbey d'Aurevilly. Barbey was criticised by fellow Catholics, and indeed prosecuted, for his collection of short stories *Les Diaboliques*, in which we see unrepentant murderers and women wreaking unpunished revenge on their feckless lovers. Yet in his non-fictional writing, there was no more effective defender of the Catholic cause. Barbey took much of his stern, authoritarian Catholicism from the writings of Joseph de Maistre, author of *Du Pape* and *Les Soirées de Saint-Pétersbourg*, the second of which popularises the doctrine of vicarious suffering or 'reversibility of merit' which is a theme of much French Catholic fiction. However, theological notions and literary creation are two different things. 'I certainly have in my head the *Soirées de Saint-Pétersbourg*,' says Barbey in a letter to his publisher, 'but I have so much else in there besides. To

---

[1] J. Green, *Oeuvres complètes*, Bibliothèque de la Pléiade, 1972-77, vol. V, p. 1367

[2] F. Mauriac, Dieu et Mammon, in *Oeuvres complètes*, Grasset/Fayard, 1950-56, vol. IV, p. 263

depict the passions, to dramatise them as I depict them, is a need of my spirit. I am dual, or triple, or multiple: all this bundle of sticks in me: too bad if the fagot catches fire - it's still me. Must I break up my being, and, of the ten thousand facets of my personality, just choose one?'[1]

Barbey, like Mauriac, like Green, had in truth no intention of giving up fictional writing. The Christian novelist loves his art. He also loves God. He belongs to two churches. To be enrolled as the servant of one of them is terrifying to him. To deny the moral implications of art, to ignore the inescapable rhetorical qualities of fiction, and to take refuge in a theory of Art for Art's sake, is a simplistic stance. As Louis Veuillot said to Barbey, 'The doctrine of Art For Art will lead you into absurdity, and then, before you know where you are, into Realism!'[2] The other extreme, the recruitment of art as the vehicle for the expression of an external orthodoxy, is equally unacceptable. Novels that illustrate dogma or exemplify Christian virtue would be mere propaganda, not art. Art, Mauriac insisted, has to entail conflict; good novels and plays depend on the clash of opposing forces, and lose their quality if one force emerges triumphantly. So Mauriac refused the label 'Catholic novelist': to a son of Bordeaux it sounded too much like 'appellation contrôlée'. He preferred looser terms like 'a Christian who writes novels', 'a Christian and a novelist'; so did most of the other French novelists who share his religious views. Nor is this preference limited to France. Heinrich Böll echoes it: 'I am not a Catholic writer. I am a Catholic who writes". And so does Graham Greene: 'I would not claim to be a Catholic writer, but a writer who in four or five books took characters with Catholic ideas for his material.'[3]

It has often been argued that one should not use the term 'Christian novelist' or 'Catholic novelist' at all, though the latter term is current in France. I would argue for its use. The looser formulations 'Catholic and novelist' dilute the compound; they separate what are intimately interconnected passions fuelling the urgency of self-expression. 'An officer and a gentleman' need not always be both at the same time; the kind of Catholic novelists who interest me cannot divide their time or, as Barbey said, their being, so easily. The term 'Catholic novelist', a term with the taut and explosive character of oxymoron, expresses best the tensions that produce the problems, and the quality, of the genre. The pull of the Catholic writer's responsibility to his creed on the one hand, his fidelity to his art on the other: this combination

---

[1] J. Barbey d'Aurevilly, *Correspondance Générale*, Les Belles Lettres, 1980-86, vol III, p. 111.

[2] J. Barbey d'Aurevilly, *Oeuvres romanesques complètes*, vol. I, p. 1301

[3] quotations from Böll and Greene in J.C.Whitehouse, "Christianity and Letters", *Bradford Occasional Papers*, Issue no. 1, University of Bradford, 1980, p. 31.

produces the same harmony as that which the French classic dramatist drew from the conflict between the imitation of ancient models and the expression of his own personality. This harmony is implied in the best definition I have seen of the Catholic novel: it is by another of the breed, Léon Bloy: 'In every novel by a Catholic, there should be an idea, a metaphysical apple plucked from the Tree of the Knowledge of Good and Evil and then laid down to ripen in the warm straw of the novelist's own individual style'.[1] Bloy has it all there: the individuality of the artist, the theological context in which he works. But this did not prevent Bloy's own novels from coming under fire from the Catholic press, as happened to Barbey before him and Mauriac later.

The problem of reconciling Christian expression with the novel as a genre has to do with the context in which the latter emerged as the major literary genre of modern times.[2] Historically, the rise of the novel and the decline of Christianity were broadly simultaneous. The novel, a minor genre for most of its history, not admitted to the canon of great classical genres like tragedy or comedy, had emerged from the increasingly man-centred culture of Renaissance and Enlightenment to come into its own as the characteristic literary art-form of an age of science. Historians of literature often assert that the decline of traditional religion and with it those older forms of narrative, such as epic and allegory, in which religious concepts could find appropriate forms of expression, had created the conditions for the novel's rise. The question was whether the novel was an appropriate form of expression for those writers who still clung to religious, and specifically Christian belief. Literary genres are, no doubt, what their practitioners make of them; but the French tradition has always tended to codify and prescribe particular genre models, and the theorists and mainstream novelists of the second half of the nineteenth century had established norms and expectations, not to say ground-rules, for the brave new genre which were, to say the least, unpromising for the Christian writer.

The dominant mode of the novel in that period was the one against which Veuillot warned Barbey: Realism. In shorthand terms, Realism was a code of writing that aimed to blur the edges between fiction and the everyday world by persuading the reader to accept that the word-picture before him offers an authentic picture of reality. That there is no such thing as one authentic picture, that we all have our subjective perceptions of the real, is the main difficulty of Realist theory, and it is usually countered by the notion of typicality, involving a contract between writer and reader based on what we regard as likely and possible in the type of circumstance

---

[1] L. Bloy, *OEuvres, 1963-75*, vol. II, p. 80.

[2] M.Scott, *The Struggle for the Soul of the French Novel: French Catholic and Realist Novelists 1850-1970*, Macmillan, 1989, passim.

which the novel is portraying. If this code is not broken, we suspend our disbelief; we only object if things occur which lie outside the bounds of these norms. What emerges is a sense-based realism, a world recognisable above all as the world we can all agree that we see. Realism represents the visible and material world, the world of physical objects - buildings, furniture, clothing: these are the things which help create the illusion of the real; and the increasing domination of literature by them brought cries of protest not just from the defenders of the classical criteria of sublimity and abstraction, but, significantly, from Catholic opinion as well, which seemed to sense that in the invasion of objects lay a challenge to the immaterial and invisible world in which the Christian believes.

The mainstream novel, then, was not just an empty form into which individual novelists could come and pour their own content. It brought with it, in its nature as a genre, a certain kind of content and an expectation of a certain kind of world, a mode of *seeing* the world that was inimical to Christianity. This challenge to Christian modes of seeing unites otherwise very divergent writers and makes Realism a coherent intellectual phenomenon. Léon Bloy went further: restating that "the novel has climbed to the empire of the world in the same moment as the virginal faith of the people has descended from it",[1] he saw the novel itself as threatening to establish a counter-religion, of which the 'Holy Trinity' (Bloy's words) were Flaubert, Goncourt and Zola.[2]

The paradox of this was that not all these Realist novelists, in their private lives, were particularly motivated, at least in the first instance, by anti-religious feeling. Reading the Goncourt diaries, or the correspondence of Flaubert, or that of another writer not included in Bloy's Trinity, Maupassant, or even the early non-fictional writing of that great bogey-man of Catholics, Zola, makes this clear. The Goncourt brothers, on the occasion of their mother's death, long for the solace of religion; then, while watching the slow and painful death of their old servant, they wonder if such suffering is compatible with the existence of a merciful God.[3] They are anguished agnostics, not atheists. As for Flaubert, he writes to his mistress Louise Colet that he doesn't understand how anyone can live without a religious belief of some kind.[4] Maupassant in turn writes to Flaubert: 'Religion attracts me more and more; it is the greatest, deepest experience of humanity'.[5] Zola argues that the

---

[1] L.Bloy, OEuvres, vol. XV, p. 72

[2] ibid., vol. II, p. 56

[3] J. and E. de Goncourt, *Journal*, Imprimerie Nationale de Monaco, vol. VIII, p. 166

[4] G.Flaubert, *Correspondance*, Bibliothèque de la Pléiade, 1973-80, vol. II, p. 116

[5] G. de Maupassant, *Lettres inédites*, Editions des Portiques des Champs-Elysées, 1929, p. 99

Realist novelist does not begin by rejecting God; he analyses the world: if he finds God there, so be it.[1] These even-handed comments, however, just melt away in the crucible of these writers' fictional works, which, in their astonishingly frequent treatment of religious themes, present religion in an invariably critical and satirical way.

To begin with, religion serves them as a foil for their own aesthetic devices. To assert the material solidity of their fictional world, things of the spirit make useful targets. The opening pages of Zola's novel *La Faute de l'abbé Mouret* give a good example. Into a country church there bustles an overweight cleaning lady. She props her broom and feather duster against the altar, crosses the church to ring the Angelus, bumping into pews as she goes, grips the knotted rope in her huge fists and hangs on it, skirts rolling, blood rushing to her broad face. For a novel about the moral dilemmas of priestly celibacy, this opening is aggressively pitched at the least sublime of stylistic levels. Ordinary life has occupied the sanctum. The altar, meeting-place of Man and Christ, becomes, by juxtaposition with the woman's humble accessories, just another object. The sacred vessels are swept unceremoniously into her zinc bucket, to be washed with her knives and forks. As for the priest's vestments, they are going the way of all matter, reaching the point of no repair. Even holy objects are of this world, whatever their alleged representation of the next.

Realist fiction is full of such ironic juxtapositions. In Flaubert's tale *Un coeur simple,* the pious old woman Félicité keeps on her bedside table a water-jug, a rosary, two combs, medallions, a picture of the Virgin, a cube of blue soap in a chipped dish: all arbitrary objects, the devotional as well as the domestic ones. Another old spinster in a third-rate Realist novel by Champfleury harbours two statues of the Christ-child for whom she has made cotton wigs, and, her most prized possession, a three-dimensional Crucifixion in a bottle, with tiny nails, hammer, sponge and vinegar flask, the whole thing animated when shaken. Jacques Arnoux, the art merchant in Flaubert's great novel *L'Education sentimentale,* offers such grotesque objects for sale in his shop window: they include this time a complete stable, with ox and ass and Infant Jesus, propped up, for authenticity's sake, in *real* straw. On a grander scale, the Jewish financier in Maupassant's *Bel-Ami* invites his Catholic business partners to come and admire his recently acquired painting of Christ walking on the waters, enhanced by the primitive cinematic effects of flickering electric light.

---

[1] E. Zola, *OEuvres complètes*, vol X, p. 1219

Something deeper than comic relief is offered by these passages, of which there are dozens in the works of the major Realist novelists. These silk-collared Virgins and wax Jesuses exude a physicality intended to subvert the sacredness of the holy personages to which they refer. Belief in a spiritual and supernatural domain, on which the Christian concept of reality has been founded for two thousand years, is shown as dependent on the physical for its expression, and in this dependence it is vulnerable. Religion emerges, in Realist novels, as the product of our responses to material images behind which lies, literally, *nothing*. Marcel, the man-servant in Flaubert's final novel *Bouvard et Pécuchet*, is seen dusting his master's wax Baptist and star-crowned Virgin, and exclaiming that there is nothing in paradise so lovely. Exactly.

All these objects are seen by the eyes. The Realist novel is the most visual of literary forms, the true ancestor, far more than the theatre, of cinema and television. Indeed, what the eye cannot see, the Realist novel cannot hold. This is the art of the seeing-is-believing age, and if ever it needed a patron saint, the choice could only fall on Doubting Thomas. In fact, just as the material order of Realism was a challenge to Christianity, so was Christianity's insistence on the reality of an invisible order a challenge to Realism, a challenge to its aesthetic, and a challenge to its claim to be a new totality, the vehicle of a total picture of the real. The notion of totality I can clarify by reference to the writings of Georg Lukàcs, who sees Greek myth as a totality, expressing all that was present in the ambient culture.[1] Christian art, he argues, was also a totality - a notion anticipated by Huysmans, disciple of Zola but later a Catholic novelist himself, who described the art of the gothic cathedral as a totality housing the mind and spirit of medieval Christendom.[2] The novel also was hailed as a totality, the frame in which to show modernity itself. To meet this claim, it had to deny what it could not show: the invisible. Mauriac writes: 'My problem with Zola lies not in what he shows, but in what he does not show. What he wrote would have disconcerted me less if the *invisible* had not been, not merely absent, but denied'.[3]

One understands why Zola went to Lourdes in 1890. The Catholic cartoons of the day picture him going there a healthy man and coming back on crutches. However, Zola was not joking. He was going to 'see' for himself that there was nothing there to see. His novel *Lourdes* is a brilliant annexation of the Bernadette story: Bernadette's false visions can be seen by no-one else, so people flock to see her instead; when she is locked away from their eyes, then pictures of her and statues

---

[1] G. Lukàcs, *Theory of the Novel*, Merlin Press, 1978, p. 37

[2] J.-K. Huysmans, *OEuvres complètes*, Slatkine Reprints, 1972, vol. XIV (I), p. 156

[3] F. Mauriac, *Mémoires Intérieurs*, Flammarion, 1959, p. 244

of the Virgin must suffice to cater for humanity's thirst for visual satisfaction. Alongside this thread in the book, Zola creates a fictional plot based on the false cure of a crippled girl, whose recovery from a hysterical condition is wrongly ascribed to the favours of the Virgin. Zola calls his heroine Marie de Guersaint, in whose name the reference to 'guerre sainte', or holy war, is uncomfortably transparent. Zola's slightly ponderous signals apart, a holy war was what he saw himself fighting: his vision against Bernadette's!

The notion that the novel was a total and self-contained universe led to another convention that was to prove a stumbling-block to the Catholic novelist: that of objectivity, of the exclusion of the commentating voice of the narrator, so that the characters, events and scenes are left to impress us and be judged by us, in theory, as directly as in real life. In Flaubert's famous formulation of this doctrine, religion again serves, tongue in cheek, as a foil: 'The novelist, in his novel, must be like God in the universe: present everywhere, but visible nowhere".[1] Mauriac, from the other side of the fence, was also to describe the novelist as God, but like the God of the Jansenist heresy to which Mauriac was inclined, a God intervening to impose his 'efficacious grace' on often unwilling characters.[2] In early Mauriac novels, characters are often halted on the brink of 'sin' - that is, the sowing of wild oats - by apparently God-inspired events that recall them to their Christian duty. Or else God's presence itself is sometimes felt, sometimes quite implausibly by an unbelieving character, but in such a way as to bring the text to a morally edifying ending. The effect, for a reader who has being following the human drama of a plot which is suddenly resolved by the introduction of an extraneous element from outside the economy of the fictional world itself, is rather like that of reading a detective story in which it turns out that the murderer was none of the characters that one had been led to suspect in turn, but a passing postman whom we have never had the chance to see and even less to suspect. Aesthetically, in terms of the reader's expectation that the novel will produce its own internally generated conclusion, the effect is the same in the *deus ex machina* denouements of the weaker kind of Catholic novel.

Mauriac altered his technical practice after his first half-dozen novels, announcing that he would instead revert to 'an indirect apologetic', from which God, as a 'fictional' character, would be absent.[3] This left all the more intact the problem of how to integrate a Christian angle into his fiction. One of his great qualities as a Christian writer lies in his insistence on choosing agnostics or atheists as his central characters, and imagining himself into their difficulties. But sometimes *his* voice

---

[1] G. Flaubert, *Correspondance*, vol. II, p. 691

[2] F. Mauriac, *OEuvres romanesques et théâtrales*, Bibliothéque de la Pléiade, 1978-85, vol. II, p. 767

[3] F. Lefèvre, *Une heure avec...*, Gallimard, 1924, p. 220

gets in the way of *theirs*. There is a scene in his best-known novel *Thérèse Desqueyroux* in which his heroine, on the verge of suicide, makes one final challenge to the God in which her family claims to believe, in their conventional and superficial way, but which she, the honest product of a 'godless' state education system, cannot. She begins to cry out in despair: 'If He exists, this Being...,' and then, suddenly remembering the local priest, a man as lonely as herself, but seemingly consoled by an invisible companion, she changes tack: 'Since He exists, let Him stay my hand before it is too late....' And at once, strange things occur: Thérèse hears footsteps, servants running and shouting; old aunt Clara has been found dead in bed, in apparent mystical substitution for the life of Thérèse.[1] The passing postman strikes again! God, if it be He who has done this, has certainly moved in mysterious ways, which say a lot, once more, about Mauriac's particular theology. But it is the switch in Thérèse's words that is most interesting, an example of Mauriac's tendency to impose his view, and his words, on that of his characters, despite his desire that they should be free. This kind of intervention, and also that of insidious comment by narrator on character of a sort that most modern novelists, to respect the self-containedness of the plot, refrain from making - these are notorious aspects of Mauriac's narrative technique, and they stem directly, as any novelist's technique does, from his philosophical and religious standpoint. More time, and more examples, would be needed to examine this question in depth. Suffice to say that this is where the tension exists in a Mauriac novel: between god-like narratorial comment and the intermittent 'free will' of the characters. Mauriac's interventions were too much for Jean-Paul Sartre, who saw no room for omniscience in a relative universe and who, developing Flaubert's theory of the necessarily invisible novelist, attacked Mauriac in a famous essay that damaged the older novelist's reputation in the eyes of the next generation. Sartre argues that Mauriac's problem is that he wishes to be God. 'But,' his essay ends, 'God is not an artist, and neither is M. Mauriac'[2]

All of this must sound like game, set and match for Realism; especially as Realism, or developments of it, remained the dominant mode of the novel. 'Perhaps', as Cecil Jenkins says, 'Realism *was* the novel.'[3] It was certainly the canonical mode, the genre model, from which other forms of novel had to take their point of departure. Proust is an example of such a departure, but even his radically new art is based on a world *within*, not the world *beyond*. Catholic writers had to find their own exit points. The novel was recognised by them as far too important a citadel to abandon

---

[23] F. Mauriac, *Thérèse Desqueyroux*, Livre de poche, 1962, p. 146

[24] J.P.Sartre, "M. François Mauriac et la Liberté", in *Situations*, vol. I, Gallimard, 1947

[25] C.Jenkins, "Realism and the Novel Form", in *The Monster and the Mirror*, Oxford University Press, 1978, p. 15

to the enemy. Bloy, identifying 'the enormous scope and potential of this utterly modern thing called the novel', argued that the novel's true ally should be not science but theology.[1] His own novels are too intensely symbolic, with characters who are reincarnations of Elijah or prophets of the Paraclete, to appeal much to modern tastes. There are Christian novelists, however, who challenge by their quality and originality the Realist hold on the genre. One is Barbey d'Aurevilly, and another is a writer I have not yet mentioned, but whose work is, for me, the summit of the Catholic novel: Georges Bernanos.

Barbey's breakthrough was to ally the notion of Christian fiction to the techniques of a genre older than Realism: the fantastic or 'gothic' tradition. In Hoffmann, in Poe, Hawthorne and Anne Radcliffe - 'femme de génie'[2] - he saw an undermining of the rationalist and sceptical spirit. He was aware of the gulf between the merely uncanny and the genuinely spiritual; but in the techniques of these writers he saw things that might be adapted for his own purposes. If Matthew Lewis could make the readers of *The Monk* shiver with fright before ghostly apparitions and bleeding nuns, why could Barbey not make them tremble in awe at the power of God or of Satan? He saw one technique in particular which was going to be useful to him, and was imitated by many of the Catholic novelists that followed him: the technique of placing, after a 'supernatural' event, a suggested rational explanation, a way out for the reader who could not quite swallow the marvellous or miraculous. In an early essay on Poe, he castigated the American writer for doing this, seeing it as loss of nerve; Poe, he remarked, was, after all, a mere Protestant.[3] But, realising for what public and in which genre he was writing, Barbey used the same device himself, so that the reader experiences both the suggestion of a world beyond the senses and the norms of a sense-based world; and is left to choose, but without the sense of unfair prompting by the novelist.

The heir to Bloy and Barbey is Bernanos (1888-1946). He is the writer in whose works all the notions I have been describing are reconciled: the dialectic of the visible/invisible dimensions, the relation of the material to the spiritual, the search for new techniques. For him as for other Catholic novelists, Realism was the negative pole from which to begin. 'There are blinkered people', he complained, 'who believe only in the realities of Zola'.[4] In particular, there was no place in Realism for an exploration of the problem that preoccupied Bernanos most, the problem of evil. For him, evil was no abstraction, but stemmed from the literal

---

[1] L. Bloy, *OEuvres*, XV, pp. 72-73

[2] J. Barbey d'Aurevilly, *Correspondance Générale*, vol. III, p. 112

[3] J. Barbey d'Aurevilly, *Les OEuvres et les hommes*, Slatkine, 1968, vol. XII, pp. 357-8

[4] G. Bernanos, *Correspondance*, Plon, 1971, vo. II, p. 523

presence of Satan in human lives. The nineteenth century, by killing the notion of Satan, had played into Satan's hands. The 'death of Satan', celebrated in Victor Hugo's poem *La Fin de Satan,* had led inexorably to the death of God, and the next phase, Bernanos prophesied in his fiction and non-fiction alike, would see the death of Man. Zola too, he said, was responsible for killing Satan: he had written that the only devil that Catholics need fear was not to be seen sporting horns and a tail, but dressed in a scientist's smock and brandishing a Bunsen burner in place of the traditional toasting-fork. Zola had also written, in his best-known novel *Germinal,* that God is dead: this three years after Nietzsche apparently patented that statement. To prevent the death of Man as a moral and spiritual being, to reassert the truth of the living God, Bernanos saw it as a first necessary step to bring to life Satan. Whatever one thinks of his beliefs, Bernanos' mission as a writer was on the grand scale: it was no less than a reversal of the modern world's intellectual development over the last two centuries or more. To attempt this within the genre that was both prime symptom and prime cause of that development, was an act of breathtaking boldness. The novelist, he declared to a lecture audience in 1926, must enter the domain to which he was supposedly denied access by the so-called rules of the genre, the invisible: 'Once I crossed the threshhold of the invisible', he said, 'I met God and the Devil.'[1] But by what techniques could Bernanos make the reader share in this double encounter?

He does so by creating, as his starting point, settings of the most banal sort: landscapes and communities that would be acceptable in the most ordinary and most typical of Realist novels, and then transforming them by showing grace and evil alive in this everyday world. Most of his novels are set in small villages in northern France, with their typical social structures and local personages: farmers and gentleman landlords, school teachers, a doctor, and a priest. It is the latter character type that Bernanos makes his own: his central figures are mostly priests. One such is the the abbé Donissan, in Bernanos'first novel, *Sous le soleil de Satan.* In personal terms there is nothing very impressive about Donissan. He is of peasant stock, more at home with pitchforks than with words; the non-intellectual priest, going about his humble tasks. But in the novel's second section, a section of great technical virtuosity, Donissan has an experience out of the ordinary: he too 'crosses the threshhold of the invisible' and meets... Satan.

Setting out on foot to visit a neighbouring parish, Donissan feels tired. He sits down 'on the ground, where the roads to Camprenoux and Vertou meet': at a symbolic crossroads as well as a topographically exact one. From this point the familiar country, the well-worn track leading past the cemetery, is replaced by 'a field he did

---

[1] G. Bernanos, *Essais et Ecrits de Combat,* Bibliothèque de la Pléiade, 1971, pp. 1078-9

not recognise, gleaming vaguely'. He climbs up a slope to get a better view, but the slope itself disappears behind him. He takes comfort in familiar objects, the hedgerows and barbed wire. But then he realises he is not alone. By his side walks what seems at first to be an ordinary little man, jovial and good-humoured, an itinerant horse-dealer. But this creature is spatially unstable; like objects in a dream, he is now on the left, now on the right of Donissan. Although it is pitch dark, he advances with confidence, pushing out of the priest's way 'the wire of an invisible fence'. He knows this place, he assures him, and does not need eyes to find his way through this darkness. He comforts Donissan, aids him when he stumbles through fatigue: then, his tenderness lurching in another direction, embraces him, kisses him on the lips, and reveals the identity that the priest has already guessed: 'You have received the kiss of a friend; I have filled you with me, tabernacle of Jesus Christ, dear imbecile. I delight in being with you, little god-man; me, Lucifer'. Then, true to his nature as fount of untruth, Satan denies his own essence; he is, he pleads, just a poor dealer in Normandy farmhorses. The text then lurches into total nightmare, as he assumes grotesque shapes, does somersaults, makes a pebble glow with heat and explode, in an exhibition as full of the conventional party-tricks of demonology as the satanic incarnations of gothic fiction.

The devil bestows on Donissan a gift of miraculous sight into souls, which is his to use well or not. However, the status of this whole scene is now questioned. As in Barbey, the reader is allowed to think that all this is happening in a dream, that Donissan, having sat down at the start of the sequence, has fallen asleep. This rational option is offered when Satan vanishes and Donissan finds himself being helped to his feet by a passing workman, who tells him that, together with a horse-dealer, he has found him lying there. Reality comes flooding back, in a cascade of concrete detail: fields, buildings, roads, are suddenly restored to the solidity that Realism would give them. Is Donissan, then, the dupe of his dreams? Perhaps; but the text suggests that the devil's temptations are real, whether they occur in waking or dreaming states. For when, in the next sequence, Donissan meets the girl Mouchette, who has killed her lover a few chapters before, he discovers that he actually possesses the insight promised him by Satan, only to use it disastrously, without charity, driving Mouchette to suicide as a result. Donissan, in another 'gothic' scene, carries her bleeding body into his church - for which spectacular offence to modern sensibilities he is banished, after suitable psychiatric treatment, to a monastery.

The devil has not finished with Donissan yet. In the final section, set forty years later, the old priest is tempted to try once more his miraculous powers, and to bring a dead child to life. As he prepares for this, he divests his person of the objects which tie him down to this earth, removing from his pockets a tinder-box, a match, a horn-handled knife, letters, a red cotton handkerchief. In other words, out goes the substance of realist fiction. Around Donissan there is, instead, 'an invisible cloud'. Of what follows we get two versions. The first is by an observer, a 'modern' priest who used to be a chemistry teacher, and who gives an objective written account of Donissan's failure to restore the child to life. This is followed by Donissan's account, seen through eyes of a different sort. What Donissan sees is the dead boy's eyes opening, only to reveal the face of 'the prince of Flies', Satan, waiting and laughing at Donissan.

In this strange and disturbing novel, a novel perhaps still, like Barbey's, too melodramatic to ultimately satisfy and convince, Bernanos crosses and recrosses the boundaries of the visible and invisible. But these two domains are still seen as two essentially separate worlds. In his masterwork, *Journal d' un curé de campagne*, he brings the two together. Grace and its satanic facsimile do not invade the everyday but are an integral part of it. Whereas Satan, for Donissan, was an exterior being, the holy personages, for the young priest in the *Journal*, are encountered within himself. His vision of the Virgin, in the midst of a period of great spiritual difficulty, arises from within, but is transmuted into a form so tangible that he feels himself taking one of her hands in his. Even the miraculous ability to read into souls, which he shares with Donissan, the power to see the contents of the closed handbag of a desperate girl, containing a letter announcing her intended flight from home and threat of suicide - these gifts are not accorded him in a spectacular encounter with the supernatural, but are an extension of his everyday faith and his life's vocation.

Again, this priest lives in a typical village, which like all villages, writes Bernanos, is prone to the modern ill of aimless boredom, compared by the priest to cancer. But if the medical term functions as metaphor here, it assumes, when the priest learns that he is dying of cancer, a literal sense that is at the same time inseparable from the symbolic. The young priest's body represents the diabolically inspired lostness of the world, which he personally assumes and helps to redeem. In the same way, his enforced diet of bread and wine, which is all his diseased body will allow him to swallow, stands for the union of physical and spiritual planes. His diet is a permanent mass, a constant communion with Christ, which for the Catholic Bernanos it would be as unthinkable to regard as mere metaphor as it would be to see the bread and wine of the Eucharist as no more than symbols.

The novel is written in the form of the young priest's diary in the months before his death. This first-person narrative solves the technical problems we saw in Mauriac.

The comments, the explanations in the text are the priest's, not the novelist's; they are generated from within the fiction, not from without. We note again the parallel between fictional technique and theological vision. The priest's diary is the perfect form for the blending of spiritual concerns with the 'thousand daily cares' of his existence. It is a synthetic form which allows the union of realist discourse and Christian meditation. Beginning as 'a conversation between me and God', it becomes a daily record of the apparently trivial events which form the priest's spiritual journey through near-despair to the revelation of God's special purpose for him, and on to the paradoxical triumph of his redemptive death. The reality of his spiritual life is underpinned by his daily jotting of apparently trivial events. The very physicality of the diary, 'these few sheets of white paper', and even the table on which it lies, enhance its authenticity, rather than subtract from it as objects would in a Realist novel. Matter is harnessed to the expression of the inner life in reparation of the Realists' divorce of the two.

This is illustrated best in the novel's central scene, the visit of the priest to the home of the local countess. Here the presence of objects is an important factor, anchoring events in the real. Throughout the intense dialogue in which the priest fights for the countess' soul against the satanic enemy, he is constantly aware of logs crackling in the fireplace, linen curtains hanging at the window, the sound of dishes and glasses being washed and dried in the kitchen. Donissan had to slough off objects to enter the realm of the spiritual, but here the two worlds are concurrent and consubstantial. This is manifested not just through inanimate objects but in the person of the priest himself. His role in this scene is foreshadowed by the role imputed to an object, to the poker which the countess is holding when he arrives. This poker, says the priest, looking for an analogy through which to explain God's purpose, is an 'instrument', ready do the countess' bidding. As the priest leads her to see that her lack of love for her husband and daughter, following the trauma of her infant son's death, is the root cause of the family's tragic divisions, that lovelessness is the essence of hell itself, he is transformed into an 'instrument'. The words he pronounces are in themselves unimportant; other words could have been substituted for them. What matters is that through the person of the priest, 'a mysterious hand opened a breach in some strange invisible wall, and peace came flowing in'. The countess' immediate reaction to the priest is violent. His revelation of her sin makes her fling into the fire the medallion containing her last precious relic of the dead child by love of whom she has been corrupted: a lock of his hair; and the priest, thrusting his arm into the flames to retrieve it, assumes quite literally the function of a poker in the hands of God. All borderlines vanish here between flesh and spirit, between the concrete and the sublime, and the theological knot of how and where grace meets free will is cut. In this scene Bernanos consummately achieves the synthesis for which he strives, the reconciliation of realism and

Christian meaning. He creates what he himself calls a 'Catholic Realism'.[1] The laws of the novel, and the expression of his faith are reconciled. He has loved his two loves simultaneously and well, and come closer than any other writer I know to bridging the gaps that I have described.

I have tried to open a number of small windows on a vast subject. But perhaps I have caused much mystification to an audience less familiar with the French tradition. Perhaps you wonder if the terms of the conflict I have described, in which the Christian novelist has to swim against the tide of his chosen genre, are unnecessarily stark. Is there, need there be, such a gulf between a fiction whose realm is the typical and everyday and a religion which, more than any other world religion, connects our flesh and blood with the god which this religion worships? I am reminded of the thesis of Erich Auerbach's great work *Mimesis*, which is that the separation of styles in literary cultures dominated by classical theory - as France's culture was - produced a rift between sublime subject-matter and the low mimetic discourse of genres like the novel. English literature seems not to show these symptoms. There is not the same tension present between Christianity and the novel on this side of the English Channel; instead, a harmonious coexistence seems to exist between Christian belief and naturalistic writing, from mystery play via Bunyan to the great Victorians. Perhaps one could speculate that a crucial difference between French and English literary traditions arises from the existence of that great work of English literature, the King James Bible, in which stories of great kings and humble fishermen are alike invested with the potential presence of the divine. There, the mixture of the high and the low is a familiar concept, and the story of Christ is itself, as Auerbach says, 'a ruthless mixture of everyday reality and the most sublime tragedy'. In France, without our indigenous tradition of bible-reading, and without a Christian form of narrative since the suppression of mystery plays in the late Middle Ages, writers had taken their tragic themes and models from the literature of Greece and Rome. A Christian fiction, and a Realist fiction, were both the inventions of a later age, and the way in which they spar and jockey for supremacy in this later age, the one against the other, is a fascinating aspect of modern French literature. As for the question of which side won, I would say that this is a battle in which one does not have to take sides, but simply to read and enjoy the works of a Zola alongside those of a Bernanos: an understanding of their polemical intertwining around common themes and images adds to that enjoyment. In the end it is literature which is the winner. Hopefully, there will also be a gain in our insights into theology.

---

[1] ibid., p. 1039

Contributors

R.S. Furness, Professor of German

Phillip Mallett, Senior Lecturer in English

P.W. Coxon, Lecturer in Hebrew and Old Testament

Michael Alexander, Professor of English

R.F. Christian, Professor of Russian

P.P.-D. Gifford, Buchanan Professor of French

Malcolm Scott, Senior Lecturer in French

D.W.D. Shaw, Professor in Divinity and
Principal, St Mary's College

- all of the University of St Andrews